W9-AVN-559

Boston Celtics IQ:
The Ultimate Test of True Fandom

David Colburn

Printed in the United States of America

Copyright © 2009 by David Colburn

All rights reserved. No part of this publication may be reproduced, stored in a retrieval system, or transmitted in any form or by any means, electronic, mechanical, recording, or otherwise, without the prior written permission of the author.

IQ Series books are the trademark of Black Mesa Publishing, LLC.

Cataloging-in-Publication Data is available from the Library of Congress.

ISBN: 1449561403
First edition, first printing

Cover photo by David Colburn

Black Mesa Publishing, LLC
Florida
David Horne and Marc CB Maxwell
Black.Mesa.Publishing@gmail.com

Contents

Dedicated to my Uncle Kenny

Introduction

THINK YOU KNOW CELTICS BASKETBALL? Think again. In this brand new book in the IQ Sports Series, find out how smart you really are about the Boston Celtics. Are you a rookie? Are you a tested, hardcore veteran? Or will you be hoping to find a team that will sign you to a ten-day contract halfway through the book?

We'll let you know.

Test your skills. Wrack your brain. It's the ultimate Boston Celtics IQ test!

Five chapters, more than 250 questions – that's what you're up against, and we're keeping score. In each chapter you'll face 50 questions in ten different categories:

- The Numbers Game
- The Rookies
- The Veterans
- The Legends
- The Guards
- The Big Men
- The Coaches
- The Playoffs
- The Fabulous Feats
- Miscellaneous

Plus a bonus question in the form of a Red Auerbach quote at the end of every chapter!

Think of chapter one as the preseason, that magical time of year when everything just feels so right with the world . . . and when everybody, even the veterans, gets back to the basics. That's what you will find in the first chapter: 50-plus questions every Celtics fan should know.

In chapter two, the season is underway and you're expected to be in shape and ready to play, so be sure and fine tune your mad trivia skills in the first chapter, because when the season starts the last thing you want is to be left off the roster. The categories are the same but the questions are tougher, and the standings count.

In chapter three, find out if you make the All-Star team. You have to start the season strong and then maintain a high level of play if you want to be on our All-Star team. Chapter three will separate the wannabes from the true stars.

In chapter four, you're coming upon the end of the regular season. Can you make a push for the postseason or are you going to succumb to the pressure, unable to close the deal? We amp it up even more, and when the dust settles we'll let you know if you're deserving of chapter five or if you will get sent home early.

You have to earn your way to chapter five. This is the playoffs. This is where you will find trivia befitting a world champion. This is where legends are made. Will you go all the way to a title or suffer a first-round exit from the second season? This is your Celtics IQ, the Ultimate Test of True Fandom. Good Luck!

Chapter One

PRESEASON

THE PRESEASON IS WHERE IT ALL BEGINS. It's the time for the veterans to work themselves into shape. It's where the borderline NBA player is trying to impress some team and earn a contract.

The new rookies are trying to show the coaches and veterans that they belong in the league and can contribute right away. These are the simplest questions that you're going to get so be sure to take advantage and get a high score!

THE NUMBERS GAME

QUESTION 1: The Boston Celtics are quite possibly the most successful franchise in NBA history. They have won more titles than any other club. Through the 2009 season how many NBA Championships has Boston won all-time?

a) 15
b) 16
c) 17
d) 18

QUESTION 2: On January 18, 1998, Robert Parish had his number retired. No Celtic wore the number before him and no future Celtic will ever wear it. What was Robert Parish's number?

a) 0
b) 00
c) 10
d) 20

QUESTION 3: The 1979-80 season was the beginning of great things once again for Boston. The Celtics recovered from a disappointing 29-53 season the year prior to finish with the best record in the league. They broke the record for the largest single season turnaround (a record that has since been broken). How many more games did the Celtics win in 1980 than in 1979?

    a) 32
    b) 33
    c) 34
    d) 35

QUESTION 4: Seven players who've played for the Celtics have scored at least 20,000 points during their career. This list includes Dominique Wilkins, John Havlicek, Robert Parish, Gary Payton, Larry Bird, Kevin Garnett, and Ray Allen. How many scoring titles have Celtics players won?

    a) 0
    b) 1
    c) 2
    d) 3

QUESTION 5: Many times when a new player joins the Celtics he will have to pick a number different from the one he previously wore because of all of the numbers that have been retired. When Kevin Garnett was traded to the Celtics he chose to wear number 5 because the one he wore with Minnesota had already been retired by Boston. What number did Kevin Garnett wear with the Timberwolves?

    a) 3
    b) 6
    c) 21
    d) 23

THE ROOKIES

QUESTION 6: As a rookie in 2008 Glen Davis helped the Celtics win title number 17. Davis provided quality minutes off the bench. He also started one game and delivered 16 points and nine rebounds. Davis, who was acquired from Seattle as part of the trade for Ray Allen is commonly referred to by his nickname. What is Glen Davis' nickname?
   a) Glensation
   b) Mad Dog
   c) The Bulldozer
   d) Big Baby

QUESTION 7: Boston has had three different players win the league's Rookie of the Year award. Which of the following Celtics never took home the trophy given annually to the league's top rookie?
   a) Larry Bird
   b) Tom Heinsohn
   c) Dave Cowens
   d) Bill Russell

QUESTION 8: Twice in team history a Celtics rookie has averaged over 20 points per game. Larry Bird has the team best, scoring 21.3 points per contest during the 1979-80 regular season. Who is the other Celtic who averaged over 20 points during his rookie campaign?
   a) Bob Cousy
   b) Tom Heinsohn
   c) Ed Macauley
   d) Dave Cowens

QUESTION 9: Bill Russell missed the Celtics first 24 games during his rookie season. He didn't play his first game with Boston until December 22, nearly two months after the Celtics season began. It didn't stop Boston from winning its first title that year. What was the reason for Bill Russell's early season absence?

a) Military service
b) Contract dispute
c) Knee injury
d) Played in Olympics

QUESTION 10: This player played in all 82 games and was named to the NBA's All-Rookie First Team in his first year. That same season he delighted fans at the All-Star break with his no-look dunk that clinched the Slam Dunk title for him. Who is this player?

a) Rick Fox
b) Gerald Green
c) Reggie Lewis
d) Dee Brown

THE VETERANS

QUESTION 11: Jim Loscutoff spent nine seasons playing for Boston. During that time the team won seven titles. He asked that the team not retire his number 18 so that future Celtics could wear it. The team agreed and Dave Cowens wore the number for ten seasons before it was retired in 1981. What text appears on an honorary banner in the rafters for Loscutoff in lieu of his number?

a) Jungle Jim
b) Loscy
c) Losco
d) Cutty

QUESTION 12: Reggie Lewis played for the Celtics for six seasons, earning a trip to the All-Star Game during the 1992 season. He died too early of an irregular heartbeat following

the 1993 season at the age of 27. Lewis attended a local Boston school before he was a professional. What Boston area college did Lewis attend before being drafted by Boston in the first-round in 1987?
   a) Boston College
   b) Harvard
   c) Boston University
   d) Northeastern

QUESTION 13: During the 1986 season the Celtics won 67 games on their way to title number 16. That team had three All-Stars and the Sixth Man of the Year. What Celtics player was named the NBA's Sixth Man of the Year during 1986?
   a) Bill Walton
   b) Kevin McHale
   c) Scott Wedman
   d) Jerry Sichting

QUESTION 14: The Celtics are known for honoring past players for the contributions that they made. Boston has retired 21 different numbers in the team's history. Which of the following numbers haven't been retired by the team?
   a) 4
   b) 10
   c) 16
   d) 21

QUESTION 15: A total of 93 different Celtics have won at least one title with Boston. Of that number 36 won at least two. The top 19 players for games played with the Celtics have all won a title as a member of the Green and White. Who has played the most games all-time with the Celtics without ever winning a

Championship with them?
a) Antoine Walker
b) Reggie Lewis
c) Rick Fox
d) Dee Brown

THE LEGENDS

QUESTION 16: Celtics legend Larry Bird made history before joining Boston by leading unknown college Indiana State University all the way to the NCAA Finals. What hometown is Bird from?
a) French Lick, IN
b) Hibbing, MN
c) Indianapolis, IN
d) Terre Haute, IN

QUESTION 17: John Havlicek was a "tweener," too slow to be a guard and too small to be a forward. He was the type of player who always went full speed and gave it his all. By what nickname was Havlicek commonly called?
a) Hondo
b) The Bullet
c) Duke
d) The Gipper

QUESTION 18: The 1962 regular season was a memorable one for the NBA. In that season Wilt Chamberlain scored 100 points in a single game and averaged 50.4 points per game overall. Also, Oscar Robertson averaged a triple-double for the whole season. But, neither one of those players won the league's MVP

award. What Boston Celtic won the NBA MVP in 1962?
a) Bob Cousy
b) Bill Russell
c) Tom Heinsohn
d) Ed Macauley

QUESTION 19: On November 9, 1984, the Celtics met up with the Philadelphia 76ers. Coming into the game both teams were undefeated, Boston at 4-0 and the 76ers entered at 5-0. With 1:38 remaining in the third quarter Larry Bird and a 76ers player were both ejected for exchanging punches. At the time of the fight Bird had 42 points. What player did Larry Bird fight with during that game?
a) Charles Barkley
b) Moses Malone
c) Julius Erving
d) Bobby Jones

QUESTION 20: Ten players have played in at least 800 games while a member of the Boston Celtics. This list includes seven players who have been inducted into the Basketball Hall of Fame. What player has played in more games than anyone else while with the Celtics?
a) Robert Parish
b) John Havlicek
c) Larry Bird
d) Bill Russell

THE GUARDS

QUESTION 21: Reserve guard Jerry Sichting spent three seasons serving as a backup for both Danny Ainge and Dennis Johnson. During his first year with the team in 1986 they went on to win the title. During Game 5 of the NBA Finals versus Houston, Sichting got into a fight with a Rocket causing that player's ejection. Who was the Houston Rockets big man that got into a fight with Sichting?

a) Hakeem Olajuwon
b) Ralph Sampson
c) Jim Peterson
d) Robert Reid

QUESTION 22: Throughout his NBA career Dana Barros was one of the finest three-point shooters. He led the league in this category in 1992 shooting .446 for the Seattle Supersonics. When Barros initially retired following the 2002 season he ranked 16th all-time in three-pointers made. He shot between .400 and .410 from beyond the arc during each of his first five seasons as a Celtic. What college did Dana Barros attend before bringing his shooting prowess to the NBA?

a) Temple
b) UCLA
c) Northeastern
d) Boston College

QUESTION 23: This guard won a title during each of his first two years in the NBA. Over his next 12 seasons he played with seven different teams, earning one All-Star selection and zero additional championships. Then he joined the Celtics and provided a veteran presence and big smile off their bench on his way to his third ring. Who is this player?

a) Gary Payton
b) Sam Cassell
c) Chris Ford
d) Jerry Sichting

QUESTION 24: Past Celtics players have enjoyed success after their playing days are over as both coaches and executives. Bill Sharman and KC Jones both claimed titles as coaches. In 2008 what former Celtics guard won the NBA Executive of the Year

Award for rebuilding the Celtics team into a title winner?

a) Jo Jo White
b) Dana Barros
c) Danny Ainge
d) Rick Carlisle

QUESTION 25: When Eddie House signed with Boston in 2007 it was the eighth team that he played with since 2003. He spent his first three years in the league with the Miami Heat. In his rookie year with Miami he married the sister of another NBA player. What NBA player is Eddie House's brother in law?

a) Mike Bibby
b) Bruce Bowen
c) Alonzo Mourning
d) Ricky Davis

THE BIG MEN

QUESTION 26: This player played six seasons with the Green and White. His biggest claim to fame came earlier in college in 1985 at Villanova leading them to an upset win over Patrick Ewing and his highly favored Georgetown Hoyas in the NCAA title game. Who is he?

a) Joe Kleine
b) Mark Acres
c) Ed Pinckney
d) Brad Lohaus

QUESTION 27: In 1980 Robert Parish joined the Celtics. A Celtics teammate gave Parish the nickname "The Chief" based on the large Native American character that was referred to as "Chief" in the movie *One Flew Over the Cookoo's Nest*. What

Celtic is credited with giving Parish his nickname?
   a) Kevin McHale
   b) Cedric Maxwell
   c) Larry Bird
   d) Rick Robey

QUESTION 28: During the 1977 season Celtics center Dave Cowens was suffering from burnout and needed to take some time off away from the team. He only played in 50 games that year while trying to clear his head. While he was away from the team he worked another job. What job did Cowens occupy in his leave of absence from the Green and White?
   a) cab driver
   b) tour guide
   c) flower delivery guy
   d) bartender

QUESTION 29: Celtics forward Walter McCarty was known in Boston for his hustle, effort and willingness to get down on the floor for a loose ball. His style of play often excited Celtics commentator Tommy Heinsohn who would frequently proclaim "I love Waltah!" after McCarty made a play. What college did McCarty attend prior to moving on to the NBA?
   a) North Carolina
   b) Kentucky
   c) Florida
   d) Kansas

QUESTION 30: The NBA first started recording blocks as an official statistic during the 1974 season. Since then there have been 27 occurrences of a Celtic swatting away at least 100 shots in one year. Who holds Boston's record for blocks in a

single season with 214 rejections?
a) Dave Cowens
b) Kendrick Perkins
c) Kevin McHale
d) Robert Parish

THE COACHES

QUESTION 31: A total of 16 men have coached Boston. This includes seven former Celtics players who moved on to become the coach. Which of the following Celtics players have never coached the team?
a) Tom Sanders
b) Dave Cowens
c) Chris Ford
d) Don Nelson

QUESTION 32: The Boston Celtics teams of the 1960s seemed to be a breeding ground for future coaches. Some of who were Don Nelson, Tom Heinsohn and Bill Russell. What former Celtics big man went on to become a Hall of Fame coach for Georgetown?
a) John Thompson
b) Ed Macauley
c) KC Jones
d) Bill Sharman

QUESTION 33: Fans remember this Celtics coach more fondly for his days as a player when he would be waving a towel around on the bench to cheer on a team victory. His two seasons as coach were very forgettable with no playoff appearances and a season where the team got an all-time low for victories with only 15. Who is this Celtics player turned coach?

 a) Chris Ford
 b) Rick Carlisle
 c) Jerry Sichting
 d) ML Carr

QUESTION 34: Rarely the Celtics go home early and don't even qualify for the postseason. Believe it or not, there have actually been five coaches in the team's history who never led a team to the postseason. Which of the following coaches never led Boston to the playoffs?

 a) Rick Pitino
 b) John Russell
 c) John Carroll
 d) Jimmy Rodgers

QUESTION 35: In 1979 Red Auerbach was so fed up with team owner John Y. Brown that he nearly left the Celtics for another team. Rumor has it that a cab driver who was taking him to the airport convinced Red to remain with Boston. What team was Red Auerbach on the brink of leaving the Celtics for in 1979?

 a) Los Angeles Lakers
 b) Washington Bullets
 c) Detroit Pistons
 d) New York Knicks

THE PLAYOFFS

QUESTION 36: During Game 4 of the 1984 NBA Finals, Celtics forward Kevin McHale clotheslined an opponent who was driving to the hoop on a fast break. The takedown caused both benches to clear and lit a fire under the Celtics. What Lakers

opponent did McHale take down?
a) Magic Johnson
b) Kurt Rambis
c) James Worthy
d) Kareem Abdul-Jabbar

QUESTION 37: On their way to the championship in 1981 the Boston Celtics completed one of the less common postseason accomplishments. They came back from a three-games-to-one deficit to win a series, something that's still only been done eight times in NBA history. Against what team did Boston recover from a 3-1 hole to win the series in 1981?
a) Milwaukee Bucks
b) Philadelphia 76ers
c) Los Angeles Lakers
d) Houston Rockets

QUESTION 38: Michael Jordan is often considered one of the best ever in the NBA. However, he lost both of the playoff series that he played against the Boston Celtics proving that the team is stronger than the individual. Jordan lost a total of six playoff games versus Boston. How many playoff games did Michael Jordan win in his career against the Celtics?
a) 0
b) 1
c) 2
d) 3

QUESTION 39: In Game 5 of the 1987 Eastern Conference Finals against the Detroit Pistons Robert Parish punched Bill Laimbeer multiple times while going for a rebound. The referees missed it and so no technical foul or even a foul was called against Parish. How many punches did Parish connect

with on Laimbeer?
- a) 2
- b) 3
- c) 4
- d) 5

QUESTION 40: The 2009 playoff series against Chicago was up and down for Ray Allen. He started horribly by making only one out of 12 shots in a Game 1 loss. In Game 2 he scored 28 second half points including the game-winning shot in overtime. In Game 6 he had his highest scoring game ever in the playoffs. How many points did Allen score in Game 6 versus the Bulls?
- a) 48
- b) 49
- c) 50
- d) 51

THE FABULOUS FEATS

QUESTION 41: Thirty-six times a member of the Boston Celtics has been named to the NBA's All-Defensive Team – an award that was first handed out in 1969. John Havlicek leads the way being named seven times to an All-Defensive Team. What Celtic is the only one to win the NBA's Defensive Player of the Year Award?
- a) John Havlicek
- b) Kevin McHale
- c) John Chaney
- d) Kevin Garnett

QUESTION 42: In Game 5 of the 1987 Eastern Conference Finals against Detroit Larry Bird came up with a clutch steal of an inbounds pass. He followed it up with a pass to Dennis Johnson who put in a layup as time expired to give Boston the victory.

Johnny Most put it something like this: "Now there's a steal by Bird! Underneath to DJ who lays it in!" What Piston threw in the pass that Bird stole?

a) Bill Laimbeer
b) Isiah Thomas
c) Joe Dumars
d) Rick Mahorn

QUESTION 43: In the 2008-09 season sharpshooter Eddie House narrowly broke the team record for highest three-point percentage in a single season by making 44.4% of his shots from long range. Who previously held this team mark at 44.3%?

a) Dana Barros
b) Larry Bird
c) Antoine Walker
d) Danny Ainge

QUESTION 44: League MVPs Dirk Nowitzki and Steve Nash are both members of the exclusive 40-50-90 club. This means shooting at least 40% from three-point range, 50% from the field and 90% from the foul line. Only six players have accomplished these marks all-time. What Celtic was the first member of the 40-50-90 club and also the first player to achieve it twice?

a) Kevin McHale
b) Danny Ainge
c) Larry Bird
d) Kevin Gamble

QUESTION 45: In Game 1 of the 1987 NBA Finals, commonly referred to as the Memorial Day Massacre, a Celtics reserve shot 11 for 11 from the field on his way to scoring 26 points in a 148-114 win over the Los Angeles Lakers. Who was this

Celtics player who couldn't miss on that day?
   a) Scott Wedman
   b) Jerry Sichting
   c) Bill Walton
   d) Sam Vincent

MISCELLANEOUS

QUESTION 46: While Bob Cousy was giving a farewell speech at the Boston Garden there was a prolonged period of silence. That is when a fan in the stands yelled something out. What did the fan say?
   a) Cooz is the best!
   b) One more year!
   c) We love ya Cooz!
   d) You're the king!

QUESTION 47: During Game 2 of the 2008 NBA Finals versus the Los Angeles Lakers a Celtics player stepped up and scored 21 points off the bench to help lead the team to a victory. What reserve player provided this spark?
   a) James Posey
   b) Leon Powe
   c) Sam Cassell
   d) PJ Brown

QUESTION 48: In 1995 the Celtics played their final game at the venerable Boston Garden. That fall they moved into the newly built Fleet Center. Since then the facility has held many names such as "Your Garden" and "TD Banknorth Garden" before arriving at its current name, the TD Garden. What is the

basketball seating capacity of the TD Garden?
- a) 17,565
- b) 18,565
- c) 18,624
- d) 19,580

QUESTION 49: In 2004 Boston held three picks in the first-round of the NBA Draft. With its first two selections Boston chose Al Jefferson and Delonte West. Who did Boston choose with its third pick, the 25th overall choice in the 2004 NBA Draft?
- a) Gerald Green
- b) Kendrick Perkins
- c) Tony Allen
- d) Dahntay Jones

QUESTION 50: Boston was very successful in the 1956 NBA Draft. Through its draft picks and a major trade for the St Louis Hawks draft choice the Celtics acquired three Hall of Famers. Which of the following players was not one of the three Hall of Fame players that Boston acquired in that draft?
- a) Tom Sanders
- b) Bill Russell
- c) Tom Heinsohn
- d) KC Jones

BONUS: RED AUERBACH FILL IN THE BLANK QUOTE

BONUS QUESTION 1: Kevin McHale was drafted by Boston with the third pick in the 1980 NBA draft. Before he signed his initial contract with the Celtics, McHale briefly considered playing overseas in Italy. This led Auerbach to say: "Let him eat" ... what?

   a) lasagna
   b) spaghetti
   c) meatballs
   d) gelato

Chapter One Answer Key

Time to find out how you did – put a check mark next to the questions you answered correctly, and when you are done be sure and add up your score to find out your Preseason IQ!

THE NUMBERS GAME
- _ Question 1:   C
- _ Question 2:   B
- _ Question 3:   A
- _ Question 4:   A
- _ Question 5:   C

THE GUARDS
- _ Question 21:   B
- _ Question 22:   D
- _ Question 23:   B
- _ Question 24:   C
- _ Question 25:   A

THE ROOKIES
- _ Question 6:   D
- _ Question 7:   D
- _ Question 8:   C
- _ Question 9:   D
- _ Question 10:   D

THE BIG MEN
- _ Question 26:   C
- _ Question 27:   B
- _ Question 28:   A
- _ Question 29:   B
- _ Question 30:   D

THE VETERANS
- _ Question 11:   B
- _ Question 12:   D
- _ Question 13:   A
- _ Question 14:   A
- _ Question 15:   A

THE COACHES
- _ Question 31:   D
- _ Question 32:   A
- _ Question 33:   D
- _ Question 34:   A
- _ Question 35:   D

THE LEGENDS
- _ Question 16:   A
- _ Question 17:   A
- _ Question 18:   B
- _ Question 19:   C
- _ Question 20:   B

THE PLAYOFFS
- _ Question 36:   B
- _ Question 37:   B
- _ Question 38:   A
- _ Question 39:   B
- _ Question 40:   D

THE FABULOUS FEATS

_ Question 41:   D
_ Question 42:   B
_ Question 43:   D
_ Question 44:   C
_ Question 45:   A

MISCELLANEOUS

_ Question 46:   C
_ Question 47:   B
_ Question 48:   C
_ Question 49:   C
_ Question 50:   A

BONUS QUESTION 1: B

Got your Preseason total? Here's how it breaks down!

SOLID VETERAN	= 45-50
SURVIVED THE FINAL PRESEASON CUT	= 40-44
HOPE TO CATCH ON WITH ANOTHER TEAM	= 35-39
BOUND FOR THE DEVELOPMENTAL LEAGUE	= 30-34
YOU GOT CUT . . . BEFORE THE FIRST PRESEASON GAME!	= 00-29

Good luck in the Early Season!

Chapter Two

EARLY SEASON

THE SEASON IS UNDER WAY. You're getting time on the hardwood, but . . . can you contribute to the team or will you end up riding the pine?

The choice is yours.

You'll need to step things up if you want to stay with the club and make a name for yourself. In this chapter the questions aren't all no-brainers so you may have to look at all of the choices before giving your answer. But hey, come on . . . if you're a true member of Celtics Fandom then let's keep it real. You should know these questions.

THE NUMBERS GAME

QUESTION 51: In 2008 PJ Brown was a late season veteran acquisition for Boston during its latest championship run. He provided the team with a clutch defensive presence, a midrange jumper, and he was a calming figure. He chose his number based on the year he was drafted into the league. What number did PJ Brown wear as a member of the Celtics?

    a) 92
    b) 93
    c) 94
    d) 95

QUESTION 52: The Celtics have finished 13 seasons with at least 60 wins. They won the Championship during six of those campaigns. What is Boston's team record for victories in a

single season?
- a) 66
- b) 67
- c) 68
- d) 69

QUESTION 53: Antoine Walker played a total of 552 games for the Celtics. He wore #8 during his first seven seasons with Boston. He donned a different number after he was reacquired by Boston after brief stints with Dallas and Atlanta. What number did Antoine Walker wear during his second stint with the Celtics?
- a) 9
- b) 24
- c) 28
- d) 88

QUESTION 54: Rajon Rondo has increased his scoring, rebounding, assists, steals, FG% and three-point percentages during each of his first three years in the league. While playing in college for the University of Kentucky Rondo wore the number four. What jersey number does Rondo wear with the Celtics?
- a) 6
- b) 7
- c) 8
- d) 9

QUESTION 55: Bob Cousy holds the team record for most career assists with 6,945 handouts. He also is Boston's all-time leader with 7.6 assists per contest. In addition Cousy can stake claim to the Celtics single-game record for assists. He set the team's single-game standard in a 173-139 win over the Minneapolis Lakers at home on February 27, 1959. How many assists did

Bob Cousy record in that win?
- a) 25
- b) 26
- c) 27
- d) 28

THE ROOKIES

QUESTION 56: In 1989 Brian Shaw averaged 8.6 points, 5.8 assists and 4.6 rebounds to earn his way onto the NBA's All-Rookie Second Team. After his rookie year Shaw played a season overseas before rejoining Boston a year later. What country did Shaw play in that year?
- a) Italy
- b) Greece
- c) France
- d) Spain

QUESTION 57: This player's rookie campaign with Boston was delayed for two years because he joined the army after college. When he did join the team for the 1958-59 season, he was used as a reserve on a championship team. Boston won the title his first eight seasons in the league with him in a starting role for his later years. Who was this player?
- a) KC Jones
- b) Tom Sanders
- c) Sam Jones
- d) Jim Loscutoff

QUESTION 58: Larry Bird was a one of a kind player when he came to Boston in 1979. He started all 82 games in his rookie year on his way to winning the NBA's Rookie of the Year award. What Boston player was the first Celtics rookie to start

the opening game of the season since Larry Bird in 1979?
a) Reggie Lewis
b) Rick Fox
c) Antoine Walker
d) Paul Pierce

QUESTION 59: In 1994 the Celtics selected center Eric Montross with the ninth overall selection in the draft. He started 75 of the 78 games he played in averaging ten points and 7.3 rebounds per game on his way to earning a spot on the NBA's All-Rookie Second Team. What college did Montross attend prior to becoming a Celtic?
a) Georgetown
b) Indiana
c) North Carolina
d) Kentucky

QUESTION 60: In 1963 a Celtic played an important role off the bench scoring 14.3 points per game and earning a spot on the NBA's All-Rookie First Team. This player, who provided a youthful burst of energy, helped them win the title during his rookie season and during six of his first seven years. Who was this Celtic?
a) Tom Sanders
b) Jo Jo White
c) John Havlicek
d) Bill Sharman

THE VETERANS

QUESTION 61: This player went undrafted in the 1993 NBA draft and played overseas and in the CBA before joining the Celtics in 1997. In his first year with Boston he averaged 1.43 steals in 61 games. He left Boston after the following season and went on to have a remarkable career as a defensive

🎁 A gift for you

Hi, I hope you enjoy this gift! From Santa

 Gift Receipt

Send a Thank You Note

You can learn more about your gift or start a return here too.

Scan using the Amazon app or visit
http://a.co/36CFq6C

Boston Celtics IQ: The Ultimate Test of True Fandom

Order ID: 110-4769671-2644241   Ordered on December 15, 2015

SDX5VT6Ykb

Order of December 15, 2015

Qty.   item

Boston Celtics IQ: The Ultimate Test of True Fandom
Colburn, David --- Paperback
(** P-1-B212E113 **) 1449561403

Return or replace your item
Visit Amazon.com/returns

3/DX5VT6Ykb/-1 of 1-//BOSS-DDU/second/7043511/1216-18:00/1215-20:23   **B2A**

specialist earning five All-Defensive First Team and three All-Defensive Second Team selections. Who is this former Celtics player?

- a) Bruce Bowen
- b) David Wesley
- c) Ben Wallace
- d) Eric Williams

QUESTION 62: Bill Russell and Larry Bird led the Celtics in two distinctive time periods. Russell's era was from 1956 through 1969 and Bird's spanned from 1979 until 1992. A lot of players had the opportunity to play with one or the other . . . but there was only one Celtics player who was able to play as a teammate of both of them. Who is the only Celtic to play as a teammate of Bill Russell and Larry Bird?

- a) Jo Jo White
- b) Don Chaney
- c) Don Nelson
- d) Dave Cowens

QUESTION 63: Red Auerbach is often credited with creating the sixth man role where a player who was good enough to start would instead start the game on the bench and come in later. Every Celtics championship team has had a player filling that role. Who is generally considered the first sixth man in NBA history?

- a) John Havlicek
- b) Kevin McHale
- c) Paul Silas
- d) Frank Ramsey

QUESTION 64: In 1974 the NBA began recording offensive rebounds as an official statistic. In the first three seasons with offensive rebounds a Celtic finished third, second, and then first in the category. What Celtic finished first in the NBA in offensive rebounds in 1976?

a) Dave Cowens
b) Don Nelson
c) Paul Silas
d) Sidney Wicks

QUESTION 65: This Celtics player was quite versatile. He was able to score, pass, rebound and play defense well. He accomplished something that has never been done by another Celtics player. Who is the only player to ever record at least 100 rebounds, assists, blocks and steals in the same season with Boston?

a) Larry Bird
b) Dave Cowens
c) Reggie Lewis
d) Paul Pierce

THE LEGENDS

QUESTION 66: Larry Bird scored at least 50 points in four different games with Boston. But, he isn't the only Celtic who scored over 50 points in a single game for the club. Three other players have accumulated 50 or more points in a regular season contest. Which of the following players never scored at least 50 points for the Celtics?

a) Kevin McHale
b) Sam Jones
c) Paul Pierce
d) Bob Cousy

QUESTION 67: The following quote is how Paul Pierce was given his nickname "The Truth." A fellow competitor said, "Take this down. My name is . . . and Paul Pierce is the [expletive] truth. Quote me on that and don't take anything out.

I knew he could play, but I didn't know he could play like this. Paul Pierce is the truth." What player said this following a game in 2001 versus Boston where Pierce scored 42 points?

    a) Kobe Bryant
    b) Shaquille O'Neal
    c) Kevin Garnett
    d) Gary Payton

QUESTION 68: Four different Celtics have taken home the league's top individual honor as NBA MVP while a member of the Green and White. There are also three Celtics who won the MVP award with another club prior to suiting up with Boston. Which of the following Celtics players never won an MVP award before playing in Boston?

    a) Kevin Garnett
    b) Bill Walton
    c) Pete Maravich
    d) Bob McAdoo

QUESTION 69: During the 2007 offseason the Celtics made a blockbuster trade to acquire perennial All-Star Kevin Garnett from Minnesota. As part of the exchange Minnesota received five players, two first-round draft picks, and cash. This is the most players ever traded for a single player in NBA history. Which of the following players weren't sent to the Timberwolves as part of the trade?

    a) Ryan Gomes
    b) Wally Szczerbiak
    c) Sebastian Telfair
    d) Gerald Green

QUESTION 70: On March 3, 1985, Kevin McHale scored 56 points to break Larry Bird's team record. The mark was short lived though because nine days later Bird reclaimed the record in a 126-115 win over the Hawks in a game played in New

Orleans. How many points did Bird score to break the team's single-game scoring record?
   a) 58
   b) 59
   c) 60
   d) 61

THE GUARDS

QUESTION 71: This Celtics guard set the NBA record for most consecutive games with at least one three-pointer made with 89 games. He went 0 for 9 in his attempt to extend the streak to 90 games. Who is this Celtics sharpshooter?
   a) Dana Barros
   b) Danny Ainge
   c) Ray Allen
   d) Tony Delk

QUESTION 72: Throughout his playing career Danny Ainge was known for being tough . . . he wouldn't back down to anyone. During a 1983 playoff game against the Atlanta Hawks, Ainge was ejected after getting into a fight with a Hawks big man. Who was this Hawks player that Ainge scuffled with in the 1983 playoffs?
   a) Kevin Willis
   b) Tree Rollins
   c) Dan Roundfield
   d) Dominique Wilkins

QUESTION 73: Ray Allen is commonly referred to as "Ray-Ray" or "Sugar Ray." Yet, Ray isn't Allen's first name. Ray is actually

his middle name. What is Ray Allen's real first name?
a) Wayne
b) Walter
c) William
d) Walker

QUESTION 74: During the 2009 postseason Celtics point guard Rajon Rondo nearly averaged a triple-double. He averaged 16.9 points, 9.7 rebounds and 9.8 assists over the 14 games. How many triple-doubles did Rondo achieve during the 2009 playoffs?
a) 1
b) 2
c) 3
d) 4

QUESTION 75: This Celtics guard played three seasons with Boston finishing with averages of 10.4 points and 3.8 assists per game. Prior to being drafted by the Celtics he enjoyed an undefeated 27-0 regular season at St Joseph's University. Who is this former Celtics guard?
a) Jameer Nelson
b) Tony Allen
c) Gerald Green
d) Delonte West

THE BIG MEN

QUESTION 76: This Celtics center played six seasons for Boston. He averaged 6.8 points, 5.9 rebounds and 1.10 blocks per game in 336 games in Beantown. But, his most important contribution came off the court in 2000. Along with his brother, this player rushed Paul Pierce to the hospital after he

was stabbed multiple times. Who is he?
a) Mark Blount
b) Walter McCarty
c) Pervis Ellison
d) Tony Battie

QUESTION 77: Pervis Ellison, a former number one overall selection in the draft was often injured for Boston and throughout his entire career. He played in a total of 193 games for the Celtics over six seasons with the club. What number did Ellison wear as a Celtic?
a) 29
b) 30
c) 42
d) 43

QUESTION 78: This player is most famous for an unfortunate incident that occurred the season before he joined the Celtics. He had been suspended for 60 days (26 games) for a punch he delivered to Rudy Tomjanovich. Red Auerbach gave this player a chance to redeem himself in Boston and he responded, averaging 11.8 points and 10.5 rebounds in 32 games for the Celtics. Who is he?
a) Sidney Wicks
b) Kermit Washington
c) Tom Boswell
d) Marvin Barnes

QUESTION 79: Hall of Famer Bill Walton began his NBA career playing for the Portland Trailblazers where he earned an MVP award and a Championship. In 1986 he was a key part of the Celtics team that won 67 games and the NBA title. What team did the Celtics acquire Walton from before the 1986 season began?

a) Los Angeles Clippers
b) Seattle Supersonics
c) Detroit Pistons
d) Houston Rockets

QUESTION 80: Five different Celtics centers have earned a spot on the All-NBA First or Second Team while with Boston. The first to accomplish this was Ed Sadowski who was the team's leading scorer in his lone season with Boston. The others are Hall of Famers Ed Macauley, Bill Russell, Dave Cowens and Robert Parish. However, only two of these big men ever averaged 20 points per game in a season for Boston. One was Ed Macauley. Who was the other?

a) Ed Sadowski
b) Bill Russell
c) Dave Cowens
d) Robert Parish

THE COACHES

QUESTION 81: Doc Rivers played 13 seasons for four different teams averaging nearly 11 points and six assists in 864 games. He never won a title as a player making it as far as the NBA Finals once. He served as the Orlando Magic coach for four-plus seasons before he was fired. Doc became the Celtics coach in 2004 and won a title in his fourth year. What is Doc's real name?

a) George
b) Geoff
c) Gary
d) Glenn

QUESTION 82: Seven different Celtics coaches have won the NBA Championship as coach of the team. Six coaches have a winning percentage of over 60% while with Boston. Who holds the Boston Celtics team record for best regular season winning percentage at .751?
 a) Red Auerbach
 b) KC Jones
 c) Bill Russell
 d) Bill Fitch

QUESTION 83: Red Auerbach leads all Boston Celtics coaches with nine NBA titles. Three other coaches have won two championships as the Celtics coach. Which of the following Celtics coaches didn't win two titles with Boston?
 a) KC Jones
 b) Bill Russell
 c) Bill Fitch
 d) Tom Heinsohn

QUESTION 84: Three people have been inducted into the Basketball Hall of Fame as both a player and coach. John Wooden and Lenny Wilkens are the first two with this exclusive distinction. The third was first inducted into the Hall of Fame because of his playing career with the Celtics and later inducted again as a coach for his work with another franchise. What Celtics player is a member of the Hall of Fame as both a player and coach?
 a) Tom Heinsohn
 b) KC Jones
 c) Bill Sharman
 d) Dave Cowens

QUESTION 85: The NBA first gave out a Coach of the Year award following the 1962-63 season. In 1967 the prize was renamed the Red Auerbach Trophy in honor of the Celtics great coach.

Three times the award given to the NBA's top coach was bestowed upon Boston's head man. Which of the following Celtics coaches has never won the Coach of the Year while a coach with Boston?

    a) Tom Heinsohn
    b) Doc Rivers
    c) Red Auerbach
    d) Bill Fitch

THE PLAYOFFS

QUESTION 86: During the Chicago Bulls 1986 first-round playoff series versus Boston, Michael Jordan was on fire. He started the series by putting in 49 points in the opening game loss. In Game 2, he was even better, scoring an NBA Playoffs record 63 points in a double-overtime loss. How many points did Jordan score in the third and final game of the series against the Celtics?

    a) 19
    b) 25
    c) 33
    d) 47

QUESTION 87: John Havlicek played 16 seasons for the Celtics. The Celtics reached the playoffs in 13 of those and won the title eight times when Havlicek was wearing the Green and White. He stepped up his game in the postseason raising his scoring from 20.8 to 22.0 points per game. He also set the team record for points scored in a playoff game in a 134-109 win over Atlanta to start the 1973 playoffs. How many points did Havlicek score in that game?

    a) 52
    b) 53
    c) 54
    d) 55

QUESTION 88: In a triple-OT postseason game that is frequently dubbed as simply "The Greatest Game," the Celtics needed everyone to contribute to beat Phoenix 128-126 in Game 5 of the 1976 NBA Finals. Due to players fouling out, they even needed a little known reserve to help out with eight points, all during the final two OT periods. Who was the reserve that scored eight points for Boston during the overtimes of Game 5 of the NBA Finals?

    a) Glenn McDonald
    b) Kevin Stacom
    c) Jim Ard
    d) Steve Kuberski

QUESTION 89: In Game 3 of the 2002 Eastern Conference Finals the Celtics pulled off the biggest fourth quarter comeback ever in the NBA Playoffs. New Jersey, which led by as many as 26 points in the game, was actually outscored by Paul Pierce, 19-16, in the final quarter. How many points was Boston trailing by at the end of the third quarter?

    a) 20
    b) 21
    c) 22
    d) 23

QUESTION 90: In Game 7 of the 2008 Eastern Conference Semifinals versus Cleveland, Paul Pierce and LeBron James squared off . . . and what a duel that was. Both players scored over 40 points. James scored 45 points in a losing effort. How many points did Pierce score?

    a) 41
    b) 43
    c) 45
    d) 47

THE FABULOUS FEATS

QUESTION 91: At the start of the 1979-80 season the NBA added the three-point line to the court. A Celtic made the first shot from long range on October 12, 1979, versus the Houston Rockets. What Celtics player made the first three-point shot in NBA history?
  a) Larry Bird
  b) ML Carr
  c) Nate Archibald
  d) Chris Ford

QUESTION 92: Kevin McHale scored 40 or more points in a game on just two occasions during his career. Interestingly, the scoring outbursts came in consecutive games. McHale briefly held the team scoring mark when he scored 56 points on March 3, 1985. How many points did McHale score in the second of his two consecutive 40-plus points games?
  a) 40
  b) 41
  c) 42
  d) 43

QUESTION 93: One Celtic player can make a claim to fame that no one else in the NBA is able to make. He led the league in both scoring and assists in the same season. This player accomplished this amazing feat prior to joining the Celtics, but that doesn't lessen the impressiveness any. What Celtics great once led the league in scoring and assists in the same year?
  a) Nate Archibald
  b) Pete Maravich
  c) Bob McAdoo
  d) Gary Payton

QUESTION 94: The Boston Celtics have had 23 winning streaks of ten games or longer. They have only had six losing streaks lasting at least ten games and actually only had one such streak during their first 47 years in existence. How many games long is the longest winning streak ever achieved by the Celtics?
   a) 17
   b) 18
   c) 19
   d) 20

QUESTION 95: Eight players in team history have recorded at least one triple-double for Boston. These include All-Stars Larry Bird, Antoine Walker, and Paul Pierce. Which of the following players never achieved a triple-double for the Celtics?
   a) Ryan Gomes
   b) Kevin Gamble
   c) Robert Parish
   d) Brian Shaw

MISCELLANEOUS

QUESTION 96: The Celtics have had quite a few players that came from the University of Kentucky. A total of 12 players who were Wildcats during their college days have also donned the Green and White. Some of the more notable examples include Frank Ramsey, Walter McCarty, and Rajon Rondo. What former University of Kentucky player has scored the most points as a Celtic?
   a) Antoine Walker
   b) Frank Ramsey
   c) Rajon Rondo
   d) Jamal Mashburn

QUESTION 97: In recent years at home games when a Celtics win is nearly certain the big screen will play clips from the Bee Gees song *You Should Be Dancing* from *American Bandstand*. There is a bearded man who gets the crowd especially excited when he is shown dancing. He is wearing a white tee shirt with a name on it. What is the name?

    a) Frankie
    b) Mario
    c) Gino
    d) Alonzo

QUESTION 98: Throughout the history of the NBA the Celtics have enjoyed great success against nearly every team. Only two of the current franchises have a winning record all-time versus Boston. One of them is the New Orleans Hornets who have won 36 and lost 35 against the Celtics. Who is the other NBA team that holds a winning percentage against Boston?

    a) Los Angeles Lakers
    b) New York Knicks
    c) Orlando Magic
    d) San Antonio Spurs

QUESTION 99: As a follow-up, the Celtics also have a winning percentage above 60% over 14 of the other 29 current NBA franchises. What current team (excluding the expansion Charlotte Bobcats) do the Celtics have their best winning percentage against all-time?

    a) Los Angeles Clippers
    b) Dallas Mavericks
    c) New Jersey Nets
    d) Atlanta Hawks

QUESTION 100: The Celtics won eight straight titles between 1959 and 1966. In 1967 the Celtics finally finished the year

without holding the NBA Championship trophy. What team won it all in 1967 to put an end to Boston's amazing streak?
   a) Los Angeles Lakers
   b) Philadelphia 76ers
   c) San Francisco Warriors
   d) New York Knicks

BONUS: RED AUERBACH FILL IN THE BLANK QUOTE

BONUS QUESTION 2: "The Celtics aren't *a* team. They're" . . . what?
   a) *a* dynasty
   b) *a* way of life
   c) *a* family
   d) *the* team

Chapter Two Answer Key

Time to find out how you did – put a check mark next to the questions you answered correctly, and when you are done be sure and add up your score to find out your Early Season IQ!

THE NUMBERS GAME
_ Question 51:   B
_ Question 52:   C
_ Question 53:   D
_ Question 54:   D
_ Question 55:   D

THE ROOKIES
_ Question 56:   A
_ Question 57:   A
_ Question 58:   B
_ Question 59:   C
_ Question 60:   C

THE VETERANS
_ Question 61:   A
_ Question 62:   B
_ Question 63:   D
_ Question 64:   C
_ Question 65:   C

THE LEGENDS
_ Question 66:   D
_ Question 67:   B
_ Question 68:   C
_ Question 69:   B
_ Question 70:   C

THE GUARDS
_ Question 71:   A
_ Question 72:   B
_ Question 73:   B
_ Question 74:   C
_ Question 75:   D

THE BIG MEN
_ Question 76:   D
_ Question 77:   A
_ Question 78:   B
_ Question 79:   A
_ Question 80:   C

THE COACHES
_ Question 81:   D
_ Question 82:   B
_ Question 83:   C
_ Question 84:   C
_ Question 85:   B

THE PLAYOFFS
_ Question 86:   A
_ Question 87:   C
_ Question 88:   A
_ Question 89:   B
_ Question 90:   A

THE FABULOUS FEATS

__ Question 91:   D
__ Question 92:   C
__ Question 93:   A
__ Question 94:   C
__ Question 95:   D

MISCELLANEOUS

__ Question 96:   A
__ Question 97:   C
__ Question 98:   D
__ Question 99:   A
__ Question 100: B

BONUS QUESTION 2: B

Got your Early Season total? Here's how it breaks down – check the scale to find out how quickly you got out of the gate . . . and the player who best represents your score!

KEVIN GARNETT	= 45-50
SAM JONES	= 40-44
FRANK RAMSEY	= 35-39
EDDIE HOUSE	= 30-34
PERVIS ELLISON	= 00-29

Good luck in the All-Star balloting!

Chapter Three

ALL-STAR

YOU'VE MADE IT THIS FAR. It's the All-Star break and you're still around. You must know *something* about the Celtics.

Can you keep it up or will you fade away and be forgotten? You're going to need to step up your game now. The benches are getting shorter, the competition is tougher, and *now* the questions start to get challenging.

THE NUMBERS GAME

QUESTION 101: Tommy Heinsohn has spent over 50 years with the Celtics. He spent nine years as a player. He had nine seasons as the Celtics coach. He served as the team's play-by-play guy for three seasons following his retirement as a player. He presently holds the role of television commentator, a position he has held since 1981. Heinsohn had his number retired by the team in 1965. What jersey number did Heinsohn wear while a player with the Celtics?
   a) 14
   b) 15
   c) 24
   d) 25

QUESTION 102: The Celtics have retired 21 numbers in team history. Many of the lower numbers are retired making it challenging for a new player to retain a number they previously wore. What is the only number between 14 and 25

that hasn't been retired yet by the Celtics?
a) 16
b) 19
c) 20
d) 22

QUESTION 103: During the 1986 and 1987 seasons the Celtics were nearly unbeatable at home. They went 40-1 and 39-2 during those regular seasons. How many consecutive games did Boston win at home beginning with a win on December 12, 1985, and concluding when they finally lost on December 2, 1986?
a) 38
b) 39
c) 40
d) 41

QUESTION 104: Bob Cousy led the Celtics in assists during all 13 of his years with the team. When he retired in 1963 he was the NBA's career leader for assists. How many consecutive seasons did Bob Cousy lead the *league* in assists?
a) 6
b) 7
c) 8
d) 9

QUESTION 105: On December 11, 1984, Boston and the New Jersey Nets played in Hartford and both teams were on fire. Both shot over 60% from the field and combined to set the mark for the best combined field goal percentage in a single game. The 130-121 win lifted Boston to a 19-2 record. What percentage did Boston and New Jersey combine to shoot in the

game?
  a) 61.5 %
  b) 63.2 %
  c) 65.0 %
  d) 65.5 %

THE ROOKIES

QUESTION 106: In 1994, a Celtics rookie scored 15.1 points and 7.2 rebounds per game and was named to the NBA's All-Rookie Second Team. He was 26 years old during his rookie season because despite being drafted by Boston in 1989 he decided to instead continue to play professionally in Europe. Who is this past Celtic?
  a) Dino Radja
  b) Vitaly Potapenko
  c) Stojko Vrankovic
  d) Bruno Sundov

QUESTION 107: This Celtics player was also a rookie during Larry Bird's rookie season. He had a solid first year playing in 76 games and averaging 6.2 points in 14.0 minutes per game. Who was this unheralded "other" rookie?
  a) Danny Ainge
  b) Quinn Buckner
  c) Gerald Henderson
  d) Sam Vincent

QUESTION 108: After playing for two years in college for the University of Arkansas this player was chosen by Boston with the tenth pick in the draft. This future All-Star started 33 of the first 48 games of his rookie season with Boston before he was traded midseason. He averaged nearly ten points per game over his final 29 games with his new team and was named to

the All-Rookie Second Team. Who is this player?
a) Joe Johnson
b) Joe Kleine
c) Chauncey Billups
d) Todd Day

QUESTION 109: The 1996 NBA Draft is often considered one of the strongest in recent history. Two members of the 1997 All-Rookie First Team and two from the All-Rookie Second Team have played for the Celtics. Which of the following members of the 1997 All-Rookie Teams has never played with Boston?
a) Stephon Marbury
b) Ray Allen
c) Marcus Camby
d) Travis Knight

QUESTION 110: As a rookie for Boston in 1998 Chauncey Billups averaged 11.1 points and 4.3 assists per game before he was traded after 51 games to Toronto. Billups went on to have an impressive NBA career winning a title with Detroit in 2004 and being selected as an All-Star multiple times. What overall pick did the Celtics use in the 1997 NBA draft to select Billups?
a) 2
b) 3
c) 4
d) 5

THE VETERANS

QUESTION 111: Seven times a Celtics player has recorded at least 150 steals in a single season. Paul Pierce and Larry Bird both reached that milestone twice. But, neither one of them has the highest amount for a Celtic in a single campaign. Who holds

the team mark for most steals in one season with 167?
a) Rick Fox
b) David Wesley
c) Dee Brown
d) Rajon Rondo

QUESTION 112: As a rookie Reggie Lewis didn't see much action playing only 49 games and averaging just 4.5 points per game. However in his next season an opportunity arose due to the yearlong injury to Larry Bird and Lewis took advantage, finishing third on the team in scoring. How many points did Lewis average during his second year in the NBA?
a) 15.6
b) 17.0
c) 18.5
d) 19.3

QUESTION 113: Don Chaney played a total of 652 games for Boston during parts of ten seasons with the club. He helped Boston win two championships as a player and later moved on to coach four different teams. He was known for his tenacious, defensive style of play. How many times was Don Chaney named to the NBA's All-Defensive Team while a member of the Celtics?
a) 3
b) 4
c) 5
d) 6

QUESTION 114: The Celtics have had the year's free throw percentage leader on their team 12 times. The current holder of the league's longest free throws made streak in the postseason is a Celtic. What Celtic holds the NBA record for the most consecutive foul shots made in the playoffs with 56 straight?

    a) Bill Sharman
    b) Larry Siegfried
    c) Larry Bird
    d) Ray Allen

QUESTION 115: The Celtics top two shot blockers of all-time, Robert Parish and Kevin McHale, are quite far ahead of the third place player. They both have more than double the blocks that this guy recorded. Who ranks third all-time for the Celtics for block shots?

    a) Paul Pierce
    b) Kendrick Perkins
    c) Larry Bird
    d) Dave Cowens

THE LEGENDS

QUESTION 116: In 1951 the NBA held it's first ever All-Star Game, an affair won by the East over the West 111-94. The Celtics have always been well represented in the All-Star Game. At least one Celtic was selected for all of the first 28 games and 41 of the first 42. Also, at least two were chosen in 39 of those 42 contests and at least three Celtics were chosen in 32 of the first 42 All-Star Games. What two Celtics are tied for the most All-Star selections with 13 apiece?

    a) Bob Cousy and Larry Bird
    b) Larry Bird and Bill Russell
    c) Bill Russell and John Havlicek
    d) John Havlicek and Bill Cousy

QUESTION 117: Twice during the 1980s a member of the Celtics took home the trophy given to the MVP of the NBA's annual All-Star Game. Once, Larry Bird won the award given to the best of the best. Which of the following players also won an All-Star Game MVP award during the 1980s?

    a) Nate Archibald
    b) Dennis Johnson
    c) Kevin McHale
    d) Robert Parish

QUESTION 118: At last count 21 jersey numbers have been retired by the Celtics. The most recent number to be retired was Cedric Maxwell's #31 in 2003. Prior to that it was Robert Parish's double zeroes that was raised to the rafters in 1998. What two players were the first to have their number retired by Boston?

    a) Bill Russell (#6) and Bob Cousy (#14)
    b) Bill Russell (#6) and Ed Macauley (#22)
    c) Bob Cousy (#14) and Ed Macauley (#22)
    d) Tom Heinsohn (#15) and Bill Sharman (#21)

QUESTION 119: Four different Celtics have won the NBA's MVP award for Boston. How many MVPs have Celtic players combined to win?

    a) 7
    b) 8
    c) 9
    d) 10

QUESTION 120: KC Jones and Bill Russell were both acquired by the Celtics in 1956. Prior to that they played together in college where they won back-to-back NCAA titles. They also were both members of the 1956 United States Olympics Team that took home the gold. What college did KC Jones and Bill Russell both attend?

a) University of San Francisco
b) Kansas
c) LSU
d) University of Cincinnati

THE GUARDS

QUESTION 121: Ray Allen was stuck in a shooting slump during the middle of the 2008 NBA Playoffs. Luckily for Boston he was able to break out of it in the NBA Finals. He tied an NBA Finals record by making seven three-pointers in the Game 6 series-clinching win. He also broke the record for most three-pointers made in an NBA Finals. How many three-pointers did Ray Allen make during the 2008 NBA Finals?

a) 20
b) 21
c) 22
d) 23

QUESTION 122: Before being drafted by the Boston Celtics Danny Ainge had a three-season professional baseball career with the Toronto Blue Jays. Ainge didn't enjoy much success with Toronto, so in 1981 he chose to give up professional baseball to instead play for the Celtics. What was Ainge's career batting average as a member of the Blue Jays?

a) .220
b) .237
c) .243
d) .247

QUESTION 123: This Celtics guard was known for his durability. He had five straight seasons where he played all 82 games and

still holds the team record for consecutive games played. Who holds Boston's record with 488 consecutive games played?
a) Jo Jo White
b) Danny Ainge
c) Dennis Johnson
d) Sam Jones

QUESTION 124: This Celtics guard was a big-time scorer. He averaged 17.7 points per game over his 12-year career including four seasons of over 20 points per game and five years as Boston's leading scorer. Who was this Celtics player?
a) Sam Jones
b) Bob Cousy
c) John Havlicek
d) Bill Sharman

QUESTION 125: Jo Jo White played ten seasons for Boston winning two titles and a NBA Finals MVP award during his time. He averaged 18.4 points per game and even upped that to 21.5 points per game in the playoffs. For his contributions to the team he had his number ten jersey retired by the Celtics. What school did Jo Jo White attend prior to being drafted by the Celtics?
a) Indiana
b) Texas
c) Kansas
d) UCLA

THE BIG MEN

QUESTION 126: In 1983 the Boston Celtics used their first-round pick, the 21st overall selection on 6' 11" big man Greg Kite. Kite played 12 years in the NBA and four-plus seasons with Boston, helping the Celtics claim the title in 1984 and

1986. What college did Greg Kite attend prior to being drafted?
 a) BYU
 b) Colorado
 c) Indiana
 d) Michigan

QUESTION 127: Celtics Hall of Famer Robert Parish was a model of consistency throughout his career. He averaged at least 14 points per game in his first 12 seasons as a Celtic. In his 14 years wearing the Green and White he had an average of 16.5 points per contest. Yet he never reached 20 points per game in any season. What was the highest scoring average that Parish achieved for Boston?
 a) 19.5
 b) 19.6
 c) 19.8
 d) 19.9

QUESTION 128: At the time of Bill Russell's retirement following the 1969 season he was the NBA's all-time leader for rebounds. Wilt Chamberlain overtook him during the 1972 season but the Celtics great still ranks second on the list. How many rebounds did Russell pull in over his 13-season Hall of Fame career?
 a) 19,679
 b) 20,308
 c) 20,664
 d) 21,620

QUESTION 129: There are nine Celtics who've averaged at least one block per game and played at least 100 games for the team, and 28 players have averaged one or more steals with over 100 games for Boston. Who is the only player to average at least one block *and* one steal in over 100 games played with

the team?
   a) Larry Bird
   b) Reggie Lewis
   c) Dave Cowens
   d) Kevin Garnett

QUESTION 130: In 2008 Kendrick Perkins would've finished third overall in the league for field goal percentage but his 214 field goals fell short of the 300 needed to qualify. What was Perkins' shooting percentage during 2008?
   a) .588
   b) .595
   c) .607
   d) .615

THE COACHES

QUESTION 131: Red Auerbach was known as "Red" since he was a young redhead growing up in Brooklyn. Very few people, including his wife Dorothy, and Bob Cousy, referred to him by his real given name. What was Red Auerbach's actual first name?
   a) Arnold
   b) Jacob
   c) Alex
   d) Edward

QUESTION 132: The 1986 Boston Celtics team is considered by many to be the greatest team in NBA history. The team featured four Hall of Famers and also contained six players who later would become an NBA head coach. Which of the following members of the 1986 Celtics hasn't served as an NBA head coach?

  a) Dennis Johnson
  b) Rick Carlisle
  c) Bill Walton
  d) Sam Vincent

QUESTION 133: In 1996 the NBA presented a list of the "Top Ten Coaches in NBA History." Of course Celtics icon Red Auerbach was included. There was also one other past Celtics coach who was listed. Which other former Boston coach was on this list?

  a) KC Jones
  b) Tom Heinsohn
  c) Bill Russell
  d) Bill Fitch

QUESTION 134: This former Celtics player faced off against Boston in four playoff series between 1983 and 1987 as coach of the Bucks. The Bucks won the first matchup but the Celtics took the next three. Who is this Celtics player turned coach?

  a) Chris Ford
  b) Don Nelson
  c) Bill Sharman
  d) Dave Cowens

QUESTION 135: Red Auerbach helped mold many players during his time as coach and GM. Many of his past players moved to become coaches and GMs. Twelve of the Celtics that he coached went on themselves to coach in the NBA. Four of them won titles as an NBA coach . . . yet only one was able to win with a team other than the Celtics. Who is the lone past

Celtics player to win a championship as the coach of a non-Celtics team?

  a) Don Nelson
  b) KC Jones
  c) Paul Westphal
  d) Bill Sharman

THE PLAYOFFS

QUESTION 136: The 1970s decade was a period that was lacking a dominant team. Eight different teams won the title at least once. Two of those teams won it twice. One was the Celtics in 1974 and 1976. What was the other NBA team to win the title twice during the 1970s?

  a) Los Angeles Lakers
  b) Philadelphia 76ers
  c) Golden State Warriors
  d) New York Knicks

QUESTION 137: Jo Jo White was named MVP of the Celtics 1976 NBA Finals victory over Phoenix. During the pivotal triple-overtime Game 5 win, White led the way with a team high 30 points. He was so exhausted that at one point during overtime before someone's foul shot he took a seat on the floor in the backcourt to sneak a rest. How many minutes did White play in this triple-OT thriller?

  a) 58
  b) 60
  c) 62
  d) 63

QUESTION 138: In 1976 a past Celtic (previous season) took his new team, the Phoenix Suns, and led them all the way to the NBA Finals where they lost in six games to Boston. He was tied for his team's scoring lead in the triple-OT Game 5 Boston victory. Who was this past Celtic who nearly beat his old team?

a) Paul Westphal
b) Charlie Scott
c) Paul Silas
d) Dennis Johnson

QUESTION 139: Among the 17 franchises that Boston has played at least ten playoff games against, the Celtics have a winning record versus 15 of them. What team do the Celtics have their best postseason winning percentage against at .824 (14-3)?

a) Houston Rockets
b) Los Angeles Lakers
c) Chicago Bulls
d) Golden State Warriors

QUESTION 140: In Game 4 of the 2008 NBA Finals the Lakers held a lead over the Celtics that appeared to be insurmountable. They were up by 21 after the first quarter. In the Finals, the last time a team had rallied to win from a deficit as big as Los Angeles' largest lead was in 1971. From how many points down did the Celtics come from behind to win in that game?

a) 22
b) 23
c) 24
d) 25

THE FABULOUS FEATS

QUESTION 141: The Celtics and Lakers have faced off in the NBA Finals 11 times. Boston has won nine of those meetings. In 1962 a Lakers star scored an NBA Finals record 61 points in a Game 5 Lakers win to give his team a 3-2 series lead. However,

Boston would win the final two games to once again claim the crown. What Lakers legend scored 61 points in the 1962 NBA Finals versus the Celtics?

a) Jerry West
b) Elgin Baylor
c) Wilt Chamberlain
d) Gail Goodrich

QUESTION 142: Ray Allen broke Larry Bird's team record for most consecutive foul shots made by making 72 in a row during the 2009 season. After he finally missed he started a new streak. How many free throws in a row did Allen make during this second streak?

a) 49
b) 57
c) 59
d) 62

QUESTION 143: On March 30, 1983, Larry Bird scored 53 points in a win over Indiana. In the third quarter he scored a team record 24 points. Since then, his record has been equaled twice. Paul Pierce recorded a 24-point quarter. What other player also matched Bird's record for points in a single quarter?

a) Ricky Davis
b) Ray Allen
c) Antoine Walker
d) Todd Day

QUESTION 144: Only four players in NBA history have led their team in points, rebounds, assists, steals, and blocks in the same season. They include Scottie Pippen, Kevin Garnett and LeBron James. The other player to accomplish this rare achievement

did so with the Celtics. Who was it?
  a) Larry Bird
  b) Paul Pierce
  c) Dave Cowens
  d) Antoine Walker

QUESTION 145: Bill Russell pulled in at least 40 rebounds in one game eight times during the regular season and three more times in the playoffs. He is the only Celtic to ever reach this mark. What is the highest number of rebounds that Russell has ever achieved in one game?
  a) 49
  b) 50
  c) 51
  d) 52

MISCELLANEOUS

QUESTION 146: The Boston Celtics and Los Angeles Lakers have a storied rivalry that dates back all the way to when the Lakers were playing in Minneapolis. They've met each other 11 times in the NBA Finals. Adding to the rivalry is the fact 24 players have played for both the Celtics and Lakers. Of the players who've worn both uniforms only one has won a title with both teams. What player has won a title playing for the Celtics and the Lakers?
  a) Brian Shaw
  b) Clyde Lovellette
  c) Bill Walton
  d) Rick Fox

QUESTION 147: There was never any doubt which side Celtics radio announcer Johnny Most stood on. He let his dislike for the opposition be heard. During the 1980s he labeled two

Washington Bullets "McFilthy" and "McNasty" – can you pick out their real names?
   a) Manute Bol and Charles Williams
   b) Jeff Malone and Moses Malone
   c) Darrell Walker and Bernard King
   d) Rick Mahorn and Jeff Ruland

QUESTION 148: In 1979 Larry Bird came into the league as a heralded rookie. When he joined the team he decided to wear the number 33 just like he had done before in college. After his 13 years with the team nobody ever wore it again because the team retired it less than a year after his retirement. Only three other players ever donned the number 33 for Boston. Who was the last player to wear the number 33 for the Celtics before Larry Bird claimed that jersey number?
   a) Garfield Smith
   b) Cedric Maxwell
   c) Ben Clyde
   d) Steve Kuberski

QUESTION 149: Former Celtics player Cedric Maxwell has served as the team's color commentator for radio broadcasts since the 1996 season. Immediately before him another past Celtic player held this role for four seasons. Who was this past Celtics player who worked as the team's color commentator for radio from the 1992 season through the 1995 season?
   a) Bob Cousy
   b) Tom Heinsohn
   c) ML Carr
   d) Jerry Sichting

QUESTION 150: The Celtics have always been well represented by players who previously represented the United States in the Olympics. Some past Olympians include Larry Bird from the 1992 Dream Team and KC Jones and Bill Russell from the 1956

Gold Medal winning squad. Who was the Celtics player who most recently played for the U.S. Olympic Basketball Team?
   a) Ray Allen
   b) Stephon Marbury
   c) Kevin Garnett
   d) Gary Payton

BONUS: RED AUERBACH FILL IN THE BLANK QUOTE

BONUS QUESTION 3: In 1950 Boston fans wanted the Celtics to use their draft pick to select Bob Cousy from nearby Holy Cross. At the time Red Auerbach wasn't excited about Cousy and his flashy style of play. Auerbach said, "I'm not interested in drafting someone just because he happens to be a" . . . what?
   a) slick hick
   b) Beantown boy
   c) local yokel
   d) home grown hillbilly

Chapter Three Answer Key

Time to find out how you did – put a check mark next to the questions you answered correctly, and when you are done be sure and add up your score to find out your All-Star IQ!

THE NUMBERS GAME
_ Question 101: B
_ Question 102: C
_ Question 103: A
_ Question 104: C
_ Question 105: B

THE ROOKIES
_ Question 106: A
_ Question 107: C
_ Question 108: A
_ Question 109: C
_ Question 110: B

THE VETERANS
_ Question 111: A
_ Question 112: C
_ Question 113: B
_ Question 114: A
_ Question 115: C

THE LEGENDS
_ Question 116: D
_ Question 117: A
_ Question 118: C
_ Question 119: D
_ Question 120: A

THE GUARDS
_ Question 121: C
_ Question 122: A
_ Question 123: A
_ Question 124: A
_ Question 125: C

THE BIG MEN
_ Question 126: A
_ Question 127: D
_ Question 128: D
_ Question 129: D
_ Question 130: D

THE COACHES
_ Question 131: A
_ Question 132: C
_ Question 133: D
_ Question 134: B
_ Question 135: D

THE PLAYOFFS
_ Question 136: D
_ Question 137: B
_ Question 138: A
_ Question 139: C
_ Question 140: C

THE FABULOUS FEATS
_ Question 141: B
_ Question 142: B
_ Question 143: D
_ Question 144: C
_ Question 145: C

MISCELLANEOUS
_ Question 146: B
_ Question 147: D
_ Question 148: D
_ Question 149: D
_ Question 150: B

BONUS QUESTION 3: C

Got your All-Star total? Here's how it breaks down – check the scale to find out the Celtics All-Star you compare with the most!

BOB COUSY	= 45-50
JOHN HAVLICEK	= 40-44
JO JO WHITE	= 35-39
RAY ALLEN	= 30-34
DANNY AINGE	= 00-29

Good luck down the stretch – time for that Late Season Surge to the playoffs!

Chapter Four

LATE SEASON SURGE

IT'S ALMOST THE END OF THE SEASON. Are you out of contention, going through the motions . . . or are you pushing hard, leaving it all on the court for a shot at postseason glory?

Could be you qualified for the playoffs already – you're just that good. It's possible. Not likely, but yeah – it's possible you're playing for a higher seeding or perhaps resting your star players for that playoff run. No matter which one you really are though, to make it this far means you must be fairly knowledgeable.

And yet, if you want to move on . . .

Well, dig deep, my friend – dig deep. Second efforts are huge late in the year and you need to give it everything you've got. If you can't do that, well, you'll go home early with nothing to show for it . . . but if you step it up, well then, that's more like a Celtic, and perhaps there's some postseason glory in your future, too.

THE NUMBERS GAME

QUESTION 151: Twenty-five different Celtics players have worn the number 20 making it the most common number. Currently, Celtics All-Star Ray Allen is wearing it. Which of the following players have never worn the number 20 with Boston?
- a) Brian Shaw
- b) Sherman Douglas
- c) Larry Siegfried
- d) Bill Sharman

QUESTION 152: KC Jones is known to the Celtics faithful as a great coach and a great defender as a player. He is also remembered for wearing the number 25, which the team retired in 1967. He is the only Celtic to ever wear that number. Jones also wore another number during his rookie year. What other number did KC Jones wear during his first season?

    a) 5
    b) 20
    c) 27
    d) 30

QUESTION 153: From 1957 through 1969 the Celtics won 11 championships, a feat that's unprecedented in professional sports. The leader of that run was Bill Russell who was part of all 11 of those titles. The Celtics enjoyed continuity meaning that many of Russell's teammates also won numerous crowns. In fact, six Celtics have won at least eight championships. How many players have won at least *five* titles with Boston in the team's history?

    a) 10
    b) 11
    c) 12
    d) 13

QUESTION 154: John Havlicek spent 16 years as a high scoring guard/forward for Boston. Seven times he led the club in scoring reaching a career high of 28.9 points per game in 1971. How many seasons did Havlicek achieve a scoring average of at least 20 points per game?

    a) 6
    b) 7
    c) 8
    d) 9

QUESTION 155: Celtics Hall of Famer Larry Bird has recorded more triple-doubles than any other player in team history during his 13-season career. At the present-time only four

other players in the NBA have accumulated more triple-doubles during their career than Bird. They are Oscar Robertson (181), Magic Johnson (138), Jason Kidd (103) and Wilt Chamberlain (78). How many triple-doubles did Bird record in the regular season during his playing career?
  a) 59
  b) 63
  c) 66
  d) 69

THE ROOKIES

QUESTION 156: Between 1996 and 1998 the Celtics made four lottery selections in the NBA draft. With those picks they chose Antoine Walker, Chauncey Billups, Ron Mercer, and Paul Pierce, three of whom have become NBA All-Stars during their career. Which of those four players recorded the highest scoring average during their rookie season?
  a) Antoine Walker
  b) Chauncey Billups
  c) Ron Mercer
  d) Paul Pierce

QUESTION 157: In 1970 the Celtics chose undersized center Dave Cowens with the fourth pick in the NBA draft. Right from the start he delivered, averaging 17.0 points and 15.0 rebounds per game. He was honored for his incredible rookie season by being named Co-Rookie of the Year along with a Portland Trailblazer who averaged 24.8 points per contest. Who was the Co-Rookie of the Year with Dave Cowens?
  a) Bill Walton
  b) Sidney Wicks
  c) Rick Adelman
  d) Geoff Petrie

QUESTION 158: The Celtics had big hopes coming into the 2001 NBA Draft. They held three first-round picks. The three selections, however, combined to play in only 85 games in their rookie season. One of them was traded away midseason, another was traded away in the offseason and the third was traded part way through his third season. Combined they only played 157 games for Boston with an average of just 4.0 points per game. Which of the following wasn't one of those 2001 choices?
   a) Kedrick Brown
   b) Joe Johnson
   c) Joseph Forte
   d) Jerome Moiso

QUESTION 159: During his rookie year with Boston in 1999 Paul Pierce finished third in the NBA in the Rookie of the Year voting. Pierce finished third on the Celtics in scoring trailing Antoine Walker and Ron Mercer. Pierce led the team with 1.74 steals per game and also amassed 1.04 blocks per contest. How many points did Pierce average in his rookie campaign?
   a) 15.8
   b) 16.5
   c) 17.3
   d) 18.5

QUESTION 160: As a rookie in 2005 Al Jefferson's playing time was limited to 14.8 minutes per game. By his third year Jefferson averaged a double-double with 16.0 points and 11.0 rebounds per game. That was the highest rebounding average for a Celtics player since 1989, when Robert Parish averaged 12.5 boards per game. What pick did the Celtics use in 2004 to

draft Al Jefferson?
- a) 12
- b) 15
- c) 18
- d) 21

THE VETERANS

QUESTION 161: The Celtics first ever home game on November 5, 1946, was delayed for over an hour. This is because a Boston player smashed the backboard doing a dunk before the game in warmups. What Celtics player delayed the first home game by breaking the backboard?
- a) Chuck Connors
- b) Connie Simmons
- c) Ed Macauley
- d) Al Brightman

QUESTION 162: There are four players who have averaged a double-double (ten-plus points and rebounds per game) for their career with the Celtics. Robert Parish is very close with 9.992 rebounds per game. Larry Bird just barely qualifies with 10.004 rebounds per game. Bill Russell and Dave Cowens are two of the others to do so. Who is the fourth Celtic to average a double-double with the team?
- a) Tom Heinsohn
- b) Paul Silas
- c) Ed Macauley
- d) Kevin Garnett

QUESTION 163: In December 1964 the Boston Celtics made NBA history. They became the first team to ever play an all African American starting lineup. Of course, that lineup included Hall of Famers Bill Russell and Sam Jones. Which of the following players was not in that history making starting lineup?

a) KC Jones
b) John Thompson
c) Willie Naulls
d) Tom Sanders

QUESTION 164: Bill Russell easily ranks number one on the Celtics in career minutes per game with 42.3. John Havlicek owns two of the top three single season averages for MPG and also had five years where he averaged over 40 MPG, yet he only ranks eighth for career average because he saw fewer minutes at the start and end of his career. Who owns the second highest average among Celtics for career minutes per game at 39.3?

a) Larry Bird
b) Bob Cousy
c) Paul Pierce
d) Dave Cowens

QUESTION 165: The 1993-94 season was a tough one for the Celtics. It followed the retirement of Kevin McHale and the sudden death of Reggie Lewis in the offseason. Boston failed to qualify for the playoffs that year for the first time since 1979, the final season before Larry Bird joined the team. Who was Boston's leading scorer during this difficult 1994 campaign?

a) Robert Parish
b) Dee Brown
c) Dino Radja
d) Rick Fox

THE LEGENDS

QUESTION 166: Over 360 different players have played for the Celtics at some point in their career. Of all those players, which has scored the most points regardless of what team they earned them playing for?

a) Dominique Wilkins
b) John Havlicek
c) Larry Bird
d) Bob McAdoo

QUESTION 167: From Wilt Chamberlain's rookie year in 1959-60 through Bill Russell's final season in 1968-69 the two players faced off in 142 games. Russell's Celtics won seven of the eight postseason series where their teams did battle. What was Bill Russell's record versus Wilt Chamberlain in the 142 games they played against each other?

a) 80-62
b) 85-57
c) 90-52
d) 100-42

QUESTION 168: A lot was expected from Kevin Garnett when he was acquired before the 2008 season in a seven-for-one trade. He delivered immediately, leading the Celtics to an 8-0 record to start the season. Diehard fans anxiously waited for the season's first game because of Garnett's presence, and a true diehard fan would remember this . . . how many points and rebounds did Garnett contribute in the team's first game of the year, a 103-83 win over Washington?

a) 16 points, 14 rebounds
b) 30 points, 18 rebounds
c) 22 points, 20 rebounds
d) 32 points, 16 rebounds

QUESTION 169: This Hall of Famer was known as a gunner, a high scoring player who played for many teams. He played 20 games for Boston during the 1979 season before being shipped off to his next team (the fourth of seven that he would play for). Who was this player?

    a) Bob McAdoo
    b) Pete Maravich
    c) Dave Bing
    d) Bill Walton

QUESTION 170: Bill Russell missed the first 24 games of his rookie season. The delay of Russell's debut didn't bother Boston though because it got off to a fast start that season on its way to winning its first title. How many of the 24 games did Boston win without Russell in the lineup in 1956-57?

    a) 15
    b) 16
    c) 17
    d) 18

THE GUARDS

QUESTION 171: Hall of Fame point guard Bob Cousy holds the Celtics team record for assists in one season with 715. He averaged at least 6.7 assists per contest every year except for his first when he finished with just 4.9 assists per affair. Who is number two on the Celtics leader board for assists in one season with 683?

    a) Nate Archibald
    b) Rajon Rondo
    c) Dennis Johnson
    d) Sherman Douglas

QUESTION 172: This nine-time All-Star and former NBA Defensive Player of the Year averaged 11.3 points and 6.1

assists in his lone season with Boston. Who is this player?
a) Dominique Wilkins
b) Dave Bing
c) Gary Payton
d) Nate Archibald

QUESTION 173: This point guard played for a total of eight teams including four-plus seasons with Boston over his 14-year NBA career. He was once named an All-Star and totaled over 10,000 points and 5,000 assists in his career. Who is this player?
a) David Wesley
b) Dana Barros
c) Sherman Douglas
d) Kenny Anderson

QUESTION 174: Ray Allen broke the team mark for free throw percentage in a season during the 2009 campaign. He made foul shots at a clip that was the fourth best ever recorded in the NBA. What did Allen shoot from the line in 2009 to claim the team best?
a) .932
b) .942
c) .952
d) .962

QUESTION 175: Hall of Famer Bob Cousy played the first 13 seasons and 917 games of his career as Boston's point guard. He returned to the NBA as a head coach in 1969, a position which he held for four-plus seasons. He even had a short seven-game stint as player-coach. With which NBA team did

Cousy make his short-lived return as a player?
a) Detroit Pistons
b) Baltimore Bullets
c) San Francisco Warriors
d) Cincinnati Royals

THE BIG MEN

QUESTION 176: This former Celtics big man also played 11 seasons of professional baseball. In the MLB he was a three-time All-Star and won a total of 91 games over his career. He has the distinction of being the only person to win a title in two of the four major professional sports, winning one with the Braves and three as a Celtic. Who is this Celtics big man/pitcher?
a) Bill Sharman
b) Gene Conley
c) John Thompson
d) Willie Naulls

QUESTION 177: Throughout his career Bill Russell was known for his defensive prowess. His ability to block and alter shots was unlike anyone else. He was very proficient at starting the fast break after pulling down a rebound or swatting back an opponent's shot. Foul shots however weren't one of his strengths. He only recorded two seasons with a free throw percentage over 60%. What was Bill Russell's career free throw percentage in the regular season?
a) 55.1%
b) 55.5%
c) 56.1%
d) 56.7%

QUESTION 178: Kevin McHale ranks second all-time among Celtics for career field goal percentage at .554. For seven straight seasons between 1985 and 1991 he finished among the league's top ten for FG%, including two years in a row where he was tops in the whole NBA. How many times in his career did Kevin McHale shoot 60% or better from the field in a single season?

   a) 0
   b) 1
   c) 2
   d) 3

QUESTION 179: This 7' 0" center out of the University of Arkansas played four-plus seasons for the Celtics. He was part of a trade to Boston in 1989 when All-Star Danny Ainge was traded away. Who is this player?

   a) Joe Kleine
   b) Brad Lohaus
   c) Greg Kite
   d) Mark Acres

QUESTION 180: This big man played four-plus seasons with Boston. He was acquired during the 1979 season, his rookie year. He averaged 12.4 points with the Celtics during the second half of his rookie season. His scoring actually dropped every season that followed with Boston. But, he was part of the 1981 title team and was used in the trade to acquire Dennis Johnson in 1983. Who is this big man?

   a) Cedric Maxwell
   b) Greg Kite
   c) Rick Robey
   d) Eric Fernsten

THE COACHES

QUESTION 181: Red Auerbach, the Celtics Hall of Fame Coach and General Manager, spent over 55 years with the team in some capacity. Most people know that he won a total of 938 regular games over his coaching career. That is a mark that stood as the league record for over 25 years. Some of those came in the four seasons before he became coach of the Celtics in 1950. How many of Auerbach's wins were earned during his 16 seasons as Boston's coach?

   a) 738
   b) 769
   c) 795
   d) 832

QUESTION 182: Jim O'Brien took over as the Celtics coach in 2001 after Rick Pitino resigned. O'Brien and the Celtics went 24-24 for the rest of the year. After, he remained the team's coach for another two-plus seasons. Who took over for Jim O'Brien when he stepped down as Boston's coach in January 2004?

   a) Doc Rivers
   b) John Carroll
   c) ML Carr
   d) Danny Ainge

QUESTION 183: Boston Celtics coaches won 17 titles when they were the coach of Boston. How many championships did these coaches win when they served as the coach of another team?

   a) 0
   b) 1
   c) 2
   d) 3

QUESTION 184: Red Auerbach was always known as someone who would speak his mind and wouldn't back down from anybody. In 1983 during a preseason game versus the Philadelphia 76ers a fight broke out. Red came from the stands to challenge a 76er to a fight. What 76er did Auerbach challenge to hit him?

a) Charles Barkley
b) Julius Erving
c) Moses Malone
d) Andrew Toney

QUESTION 185: Alvin Julian was the second coach in the Celtics history. Prior to his two-year stint with Boston he coached Bob Cousy and Holy Cross. After leaving the Celtics Julian coached at Dartmouth for 17 years. By what nickname was Alvin Julian commonly known?

a) Doggie
b) The Jewel
c) The Whistler
d) Flip

THE PLAYOFFS

QUESTION 186: The 1969 NBA Finals of Boston versus the Los Angeles Lakers went the full seven games. In Game 7 a Celtics player stepped up late to hit a clutch shot that hit the rim and bounced high in the air before it went through the hoop. What Celtics player hit a shot to secure the Game 7 win and Boston's 11th title?

a) Don Nelson
b) Sam Jones
c) Bill Russell
d) Bailey Howell

QUESTION 187: The Celtics are known across the NBA and all professional sports for bringing home the title ... well, *multiple titles*. They have beaten a total of seven different teams in the NBA Finals with the Los Angeles Lakers being their most common victim. What franchise have the Celtics beaten the second most times in the NBA Finals?

a) Houston Rockets
b) Golden State Warriors
c) Phoenix Suns
d) Atlanta Hawks

QUESTION 188: The NBA began giving away an NBA Finals MVP award beginning with the 1969 Finals. In 1969 the Celtics beat the Lakers in seven games. Who was the first recipient of the NBA Finals MVP award in 1969?

a) Bill Russell
b) John Havlicek
c) Jerry West
d) Sam Jones

QUESTION 189: On April 28, 1990, the Celtics achieved their biggest offensive output ever in a single playoff game against the New York Knicks. They gave up 128 points and still won the game. Unfortunately, they would go on to lose the series. What is the most points that the Celtics ever scored in a postseason game?

a) 150
b) 153
c) 155
d) 157

QUESTION 190: In Game 6 of the 2008 NBA Finals the Celtics beat the Lakers 131-92 to close out the series. The 39-point win was the largest margin of victory in NBA Finals history and the Celtics second largest win ever in the playoffs. In 1982 the Celtics won a postseason game by 40 points. Against what team did Boston earn its 40-point victory?

a) Philadelphia 76ers
b) Atlanta Hawks
c) Milwaukee Bucks
d) Los Angeles Lakers

THE FABULOUS FEATS

QUESTION 191: In 1996 the NBA announced a list of the "Top Ten Teams in NBA History." The list included two Celtics teams. One was the great 1985-86 squad that won 67 games on its way to its 16th NBA Championship. What was the other Boston team that was named one of the ten-best of all-time?

a) 1961-62
b) 1983-84
c) 1959-60
d) 1964-65

QUESTION 192: Wilt Chamberlain and Bill Russell are unquestionably the top two rebounders in the history of the NBA. Their rebounding dominance extends to the postseason as well. Russell and Chamberlain combined own the top 11 rebounding games in postseason history. Russell twice recorded the top rebounding total in NBA Finals history. How many rebounds did Bill Russell pull down in a single game on two occasions to set the NBA Finals mark?

a) 38
b) 40
c) 42
d) 44

QUESTION 193: In 1958 during Bill Russell's first full season in the NBA he averaged over 20 rebounds per game, something that had never been done before in NBA history. He would go on to accomplish this feat many times. How many times during his career did Bill Russell average at least 20 rebounds per game for a full season?

   a) 8
   b) 9
   c) 10
   d) 11

QUESTION 194: It isn't always a Celtics player who enjoys a great game when the Celtics play. Sometimes it's a Celtics opponent who has a memorable showing. Who's the last Celtics opponent to score 50 or more points against Boston?

   a) Hakeem Olajuwon
   b) Kobe Bryant
   c) Michael Jordan
   d) David Robinson

QUESTION 195: The Celtics have had some of the greatest free throw shooters in NBA history. These include Bill Sharman, Larry Siegfried, Larry Bird, and Ray Allen. A Celtic has led the league in free throw percentage 13 times. The 1990 Boston Celtics team set the NBA record for best foul shooting by a team over a season. What percentage did the 1990 Celtics shoot on their way to setting a new free throw percentage mark?

   a) .824
   b) .828
   c) .832
   d) .836

MISCELLANEOUS

QUESTION 196: Boston has had numerous Hall of Famers and All-Stars play for them. This might make you think that they've had the first pick in the NBA draft many times in order to acquire those great talents. Actually, only once did the Celtics make the first overall pick in the entire draft. Who was the player selected by Boston the only time it made the top selection in the draft?

a) Bill Russell
b) Len Bias
c) Charlie Share
d) Dave Cowens

QUESTION 197: The Boston Celtics have been littered with great players throughout their existence. At last count 33 men with an association with the team have been inducted into the Basketball Hall of Fame. Plus, there are others who will some day be enshrined as well. Boston has had a total of 77 selections to the All-NBA teams that are selected each year. Who was the first Celtics player to be chosen to an All-NBA team?

a) Bob Cousy
b) Ed Macauley
c) Ed Sadowski
d) Bill Sharman

QUESTION 198: Johnny Most was long known as the voice of the Boston Celtics calling the team's radio broadcasts for 37 seasons. It's hard to remember a play without also remembering how Most called it. He was a very strong supporter of Boston and let his distaste for the opposition be heard. What was Johnny Most's first season as the play-by-play announcer for Boston's radio broadcasts?

a) 1952-53
b) 1953-54
c) 1954-55
d) 1955-56

QUESTION 199: Twenty times in their history the Celtics have won by 40 points or more. Interestingly, their three biggest

margins of victory, 51 points, 49 points, and 48 points all came against the same franchise. Against what team did the Celtics record the three biggest wins in their history?
   a) Lakers
   b) 76ers
   c) Warriors
   d) Knicks

QUESTION 200: In the 1978 NBA Draft the Celtics had two first-round picks. They used the sixth overall selection to choose Larry Bird. Who did the Celtics also select in the first-round of the 1978 NBA Draft with the eighth pick?
   a) Danny Ainge
   b) Freeman Williams
   c) Norm Cook
   d) Cedric Maxwell

BONUS: RED AUERBACH FILL IN THE BLANK QUOTE

BONUS QUESTION 4: "Individual honors are nice, but no Celtic has gone out of his way to achieve them. We have never had the league's top scorer. In fact, we won seven league championships without placing even one among the league's top ten scorers. Our pride was never rooted in" . . . what?
   a) statistics
   b) awards
   c) individuals
   d) accolades

Chapter Four Answer Key

Time to find out how you did – put a check mark next to the questions you answered correctly, and when you are done be sure and add up your score to find out your Late Season Surge IQ!

THE NUMBERS GAME
_ Question 151: D
_ Question 152: C
_ Question 153: B
_ Question 154: C
_ Question 155: A

THE ROOKIES
_ Question 156: A
_ Question 157: D
_ Question 158: D
_ Question 159: B
_ Question 160: B

THE VETERANS
_ Question 161: A
_ Question 162: B
_ Question 163: B
_ Question 164: D
_ Question 165: B

THE LEGENDS
_ Question 166: A
_ Question 167: B
_ Question 168: C
_ Question 169: A
_ Question 170: B

THE GUARDS
_ Question 171: D
_ Question 172: C
_ Question 173: D
_ Question 174: C
_ Question 175: D

THE BIG MEN
_ Question 176: B
_ Question 177: C
_ Question 178: C
_ Question 179: A
_ Question 180: C

THE COACHES
_ Question 181: C
_ Question 182: B
_ Question 183: A
_ Question 184: C
_ Question 185: A

THE PLAYOFFS
_ Question 186: A
_ Question 187: D
_ Question 188: C
_ Question 189: D
_ Question 190: A

THE FABULOUS FEATS
    _ Question 191: D
    _ Question 192: B
    _ Question 193: C
    _ Question 194: A
    _ Question 195: C

MISCELLANEOUS
    _ Question 196: C
    _ Question 197: C
    _ Question 198: B
    _ Question 199: C
    _ Question 200: B

BONUS QUESTION 4: A

Got your Late Season Surge total? Here's how it breaks down – check the scale to find out how well you carried the club down the stretch . . . and the player who best represents your score!

BILL RUSSELL	= 45-50
LARRY BIRD	= 40-44
PAUL PIERCE	= 35-39
DENNIS JOHNSON	= 30-34
BRIAN SCALABRINE	= 00-29

Good luck in the Playoffs!

Chapter Five

PLAYOFFS

IT ALL COMES DOWN TO THIS. You spent your childhood dreaming of this moment.

You've made it to the postseason.

It took skill, cunning, and most importantly, extraordinary amounts of raw nerve and pure knowledge to get this far. And now . . . well, everyone's watching.

This is where legends are made, but if you rest on your past accomplishments you might as well be done – you won't be bringing home any hardware. You need your 'A' game and then some if you want the big prize.

Did you think some of the questions that got you to this point were hard? If so, you were wrong. *Now* they get hard. Think you have what it takes? Are you going to win it all like Bill Russell or are you out of luck, like, oh I don't know, let's say . . . the *Clippers*.

Well, are you?

There's only one way to find out – let's do this!

THE NUMBERS GAME

QUESTION 201: The Boston Garden served as the Celtics home for nearly 50 years. It was known for its distinctive features (or lack thereof) that often provided the home team with an edge. The distinctive parquet was rumored to have "dead spots" that Celtics players knew about and could take advantage of. How many bolts were used to hold the panels of the parquet floor in place?

a) 968
b) 988
c) 1,000
d) 1,008

QUESTION 202: Over time Celtics fans have become accustomed to seeing their team finish first. Boston has won its division a total of 27 times. What is the most number of games more than the second place team that Boston has finished ahead?

a) 19
b) 21
c) 25
d) 26

QUESTION 203: Larry Bird's final triple-double may have been his best. In a double-overtime 152-148 win over Portland on March 15, 1992, Bird finished with 14 rebounds and 12 assists. He also set the record for the most points scored by a player in a game in which he netted a triple-double. How many points did Bird score in his final triple-double contest?

a) 47
b) 49
c) 51
d) 52

QUESTION 204: The "Jones Boys" were a fixture of the Celtics championship winning teams of the 1960s. KC and Sam were teammates for KC's entire nine-year career. They weren't the only Joneses to play for the Celtics. How many players with the

last name "Jones" have played in games for Boston?
a) 5
b) 6
c) 7
d) 8

QUESTION 205: Robert Parish played an NBA record 1,611 games in 21 seasons. He played 14 of those years with Boston. How many games did Parish play for the Celtics?
a) 1,028
b) 1,106
c) 1,128
d) 1,160

THE ROOKIES

QUESTION 206: Kevin McHale holds the team's rookie record for blocks with 151 during the 1981 season. What player is next with 76 blocks, just barely more than half of McHale's total?
a) Al Jefferson
b) Kendrick Perkins
c) Eric Montross
d) Mark Blount

QUESTION 207: In the 1978 NBA draft Larry Bird was chosen with the sixth overall pick as a junior eligible. Only two of the five players chosen before him were named to the NBA's All-Rookie Team. How many All-Star selections did those five top-five selections combine to earn during their careers?
a) 0
b) 4
c) 8
d) 12

QUESTION 208: As a rookie in 1970 Jo Jo White averaged 12.2 points per game and was named to the NBA's All-Rookie Team. Over the next seven years he averaged between 18.1 and 23.1 points per game every year. How many seasons was Jo Jo White Boston's leading scorer?
  a) 1
  b) 2
  c) 3
  d) 4

QUESTION 209: In 1957 Boston selected North Carolina Central guard Sam Jones with the eighth overall selection. In his rookie year he had the lowest scoring average of his career. The team didn't win the title that year. Boston did win the title in ten of his final 11 years. How many points did Jones average during his rookie season?
  a) 4.6
  b) 5.8
  c) 6.3
  d) 7.8

QUESTION 210: In 1971 Dave Cowens of the Celtics was named Co-Rookie of the Year. The following three seasons the award was won by a non-Celtic who would later play for Boston. Which of the following Rookie of the Year winners didn't win between 1972 and 1974 and later play with the Celtics?
  a) Jamaal Wilkes
  b) Bob McAdoo
  c) Ernie DiGregorio
  d) Sidney Wicks

THE VETERANS

QUESTION 211: A Celtics player has never scored at least 40 points in a game against the Toronto Raptors. Paul Pierce comes the closest with a 39-point showing. A former Celtic holds the Raptors record for most points scored in a game versus Boston with 40. Who is the past Celtic?

a) Acie Earl
b) Dee Brown
c) Eric Williams
d) Eric Montross

QUESTION 212: In 2003 Antoine Walker was traded with another Celtic to the Dallas Mavericks. After the season Walker was traded with that same player again, this time landing in Atlanta. Who was the other past Celtic who was twice traded with Antoine Walker?

a) Bimbo Coles
b) Raef LaFrentz
c) Adrian Griffin
d) Tony Delk

QUESTION 213: This one-time All-Star played three seasons with Boston, averaging as much as 13.2 points per game. While in college he was the first player to lead the country in both scoring and rebounding in the same season. Hank Gathers later accomplished it as well. Who is this former Celtic?

a) Paul Silas
b) Sidney Wicks
c) Raef LaFrentz
d) Xavier McDaniel

QUESTION 214: In 1946 the Celtics began play in the BAA. After three seasons they joined the NBA when the BAA and NBL merged. Who was the Celtics leading scorer in their initial

1946-47 season with 10.3 points per game?
 a) Al Brightman
 b) Ed Sadowski
 c) Connie Simmons
 d) Mel Riebe

QUESTION 215: Five different players have fouled out of over 50 games while playing for the Celtics. The team's all-time leader finished with 94 DQs and also has the team's single season record with 19 DQs. What Celtic holds both the team's career and single season records for games fouled out of?
 a) Dave Cowens
 b) Frank Ramsey
 c) Tom Sanders
 d) John Havlicek

THE LEGENDS

QUESTION 216: Dave Cowens played the first ten seasons of his Hall of Fame career with the Celtics. He retired following the 1980 season. He came out of retirement to play 40 games during the 1983 season. What team did Cowens play for in 1983 before retiring for good?
 a) Philadelphia 76ers
 b) Milwaukee Bucks
 c) New York Knicks
 d) Detroit Pistons

QUESTION 217: The Celtics have had many great scorers play for them. However, some had their biggest scoring years before they joined Boston. Which former Celtic has the highest career scoring average (including games not with the Celtics) at 24.8

points per game?
a) Larry Bird
b) Bob McAdoo
c) Pete Maravich
d) Dominique Wilkins

QUESTION 218: Larry Bird achieved a triple-double in only three quarters of play on February 18, 1985. He finished with 30 points, 12 rebounds, and 10 assists. He also had a team record nine steals. He didn't play at all in the fourth quarter because Boston led by 24 points after the third. What team did Bird record this three-quarter triple-double, which was also nearly a quadruple double?
a) Phoenix Suns
b) Los Angeles Clippers
c) Cleveland Cavaliers
d) Utah Jazz

QUESTION 219: Bob Cousy was drafted with the third overall pick in the 1950 NBA Draft. After he refused to report to the team that drafted him he was traded to the Chicago Stags. The Stags franchise folded and then he was awarded to Boston in the dispersal draft. What was the team that initially drafted Bob Cousy?
a) Tri-Cities Blackhawks
b) Fort Wayne Pistons
c) Philadelphia Warriors
d) Rochester Royals

QUESTION 220: At the time of the 1956 NBA Draft the Celtics completed a historical trade that brought them the second overall pick Bill Russell. The Celtics had to give up future Hall of Famer Ed Macauley who had spent the first six years of his career starring for Boston. They also had to trade their third-round selection from the 1953 NBA Draft who was also later

inducted into the Hall of Fame. Who was the second player included in the Celtics trade for Bill Russell?
  a) Gene Conley
  b) Arnold Risen
  c) Cliff Hagan
  d) Andy Phillip

THE GUARDS

QUESTION 221: In 1982 Dave Cowens decided to come out of retirement to play for his former teammate Don Nelson. The Celtics still owned Cowens' rights so they received a guard in return. This player was part of Boston's championship winning squad in 1984. What Celtics guard was acquired in a trade for Dave Cowens?
  a) Dennis Johnson
  b) Gerald Henderson
  c) Quinn Buckner
  d) Carlos Clark

QUESTION 222: This former Celtic actually averaged more assists than points over his 137-game, three-year stint with Boston. A 6' 0" point guard who averaged 5.8 assists and 5.7 points in his stay, who is he?
  a) David Wesley
  b) Kenny Anderson
  c) Delonte West
  d) John Bagley

QUESTION 223: Tony Delk played for eight different teams in his ten-season NBA career. He averaged 9.2 points per game in one-plus seasons with the Celtics. Delk was acquired by Boston from Phoenix in 2002 along with another player for the stretch run and playoffs. Who was the other player that was obtained

in the trade with Phoenix?
  a) Grant Long
  b) Rodney Rogers
  c) Bryant Stith
  d) Randy Brown

QUESTION 224: Bob Cousy is the Celtics all-time leader for both assists and assists per game accumulating 6,945 handouts and an average of 7.6 assists per contest. Who holds the second highest career assists per game mark in team history?
  a) Rajon Rondo
  b) Larry Bird
  c) Dennis Johnson
  d) Nate Archibald

QUESTION 225: Dennis Johnson was known throughout his career as a clutch player who played great defense. He was named the NBA Finals MVP with Seattle in 1979. How many times in his 14-year career was Johnson named to the NBA's All-Defensive Teams?
  a) 6
  b) 7
  c) 8
  d) 9

THE BIG MEN

QUESTION 226: On January 21, 1983, the Celtics set a team record for blocked shots in a 117-106 win at Chicago. Kevin McHale led the way with nine rejections, a mark that tied the team record that was previously shared by himself and Robert Parish. How many shots did Boston swat away to break the

team record for blocks in a single contest?
a) 15
b) 16
c) 17
d) 18

QUESTION 227: Raef LaFrentz, the 6' 11" big man was always something of an oddity, a center that was most comfortable shooting from long range. He made 82 three's in 2005 and 112 in 2006 for Boston. What was LaFrentz's three-point shooting percentage during the 2006 season?
a) .388
b) .392
c) .398
d) .402

QUESTION 228: This five-time All-Star earned his way into the Hall of Fame as a GM. He played two seasons with Boston as a backup to Bill Russell. Who is this Hall of Fame GM?
a) Bill Sharman
b) John Thompson
c) Don Nelson
d) Wayne Embry

QUESTION 229: Big men usually accumulate fouls more frequently than smaller players. Every player to lead the league in fouls since 1975 has been at least 6' 5" and most were at least 6' 9". Interestingly, the player who played the most games for Boston without fouling out is a center. What Celtics player played in the most games for the Celtics without ever fouling out?
a) Eric Fernsten
b) Brett Szabo
c) Alton Lister
d) Joe Kleine

QUESTION 230: In 1964 the Celtics selected a 7' 0" center out of Oregon State with the ninth overall pick. He played two years for Boston winning two titles followed by ten seasons with five other teams that resulted in zero championships. Who is he?
a) Mel Counts
b) Jim Loscutoff
c) Clyde Lovellette
d) Tom Sanders

THE COACHES

QUESTION 231: Six different Celtics coaches have served as the Eastern Conference's coach for the All-Star Game. Five of those coaches won a title as Boston's head man. How many All-Star Games have been coached by the Celtics top man?
a) 19
b) 20
c) 21
d) 22

QUESTION 232: Red Auerbach enjoyed success with the Celtics and before he was with them. Only one team, the Anderson Packers, a team that existed for only one season before folding, had a winning record against him. Against which current franchise did Auerbach record his best winning percentage as coach?
a) Boston Celtics
b) Washington Wizards
c) Los Angeles Lakers
d) New York Knicks

QUESTION 233: Former Celtic great Bob Cousy became a coach following his retirement from the team in 1963. What team did

Cousy coach in 1963?
a) Boston College
b) Los Angeles Lakers
c) Cincinnati Royals
d) Holy Cross

QUESTION 234: Bill Fitch was an NBA coach for 26 seasons. His winning percentage for his four years with the Celtics was an incredible 73.8%. Interestingly, his winning percentage for the other 22 years of his career was only 40.8%. How many regular season victories did Fitch earn during his NBA coaching career?
a) 908
b) 938
c) 944
d) 1,006

QUESTION 235: The Celtics first started play in 1946 as an initial member of the Basketball Association of America (BAA), a precursor to the NBA. The Celtics didn't enjoy much success immediately. They actually didn't achieve their first winning record until their fifth season when they hired an energetic young coach Red Auerbach. What was Boston's record during its initial year in 1946-47?
a) 22–38
b) 24–36
c) 25–35
d) 27–33

THE PLAYOFFS

QUESTION 236: In 1965 during Game 7 of the Eastern Conference Finals versus Philadelphia "Havlicek stole the ball!" and the Celtics won the game and the series to advance to the Finals. Boston went on to win its seventh consecutive title by defeating the Los Angeles Lakers. What 76ers player threw the inbounds pass that Havlicek stole?

a) Wilt Chamberlain
b) Luke Jackson
c) Chet Walker
d) Hal Greer

QUESTION 237: Three times in their history the Boston Celtics have reached the NBA Finals in the same year that the Boston Bruins reached the NHL's Stanley Cup Finals. The first time this happened was in 1957. It also happened the next season when both again reached their sport's championship round. What was the third season during which both the Boston Celtics and Boston Bruins advanced to the Championship of their sport?

a) 1959
b) 1969
c) 1974
d) 1987

QUESTION 238: During the 1976 NBA Finals one Celtics player fouled out of five of the six games and received five fouls in the other game. He fouled out of 11 of the 18 postseason games that year averaging 5.4 fouls per contest. What player was this?

a) John Havlicek
b) Dave Cowens
c) Charlie Scott
d) Paul Silas

QUESTION 239: In 1983 the Celtics were swept 4-0 in the Eastern Conference Finals to a team coached by a former Celtics player. The disappointing result led to the firing of

Celtics coach Bill Fitch. What team swept Boston in the 1983 postseason?

    a) Philadelphia 76ers
    b) Milwaukee Bucks
    c) Atlanta Hawks
    d) Washington Bullets

QUESTION 240: The Celtics have played in a seventh and deciding game in 26 playoff series. They are 7-0 all-time when they play in Game 7 of the NBA Finals. By comparison, the Los Angeles Lakers are 3-5. How many of the 26 series deciders were won by the Celtics?

    a) 17
    b) 18
    c) 19
    d) 20

THE FABULOUS FEATS

QUESTION 241: On March 4, 2007, the Celtics beat the Timberwolves 124-117 in double-overtime. A Celtic scored 31 points with all of them coming after halftime. The 15 points that he scored in the overtimes broke the team's record. Who is this Celtic who owns the team record for most points scored during overtime in one game?

    a) Delonte West
    b) Paul Pierce
    c) Al Jefferson
    d) Wally Szczerbiak

QUESTION 242: During the 1990-91 season Boston tied an NBA record by having six players score at least 1,000 points. Three of them are easy, the "Big Three" (Bird, McHale, and Parish).

Which of following players didn't score 1,000 points for Boston that season?
   a) Reggie Lewis
   b) Dee Brown
   c) Kevin Gamble
   d) Brian Shaw

QUESTION 243: Six times in team history a Celtic has led the entire league in field goal percentage. Four different players have accomplished this including two straight seasons by Kevin McHale. Which of the following Celtics never led the league in field goal percentage?
   a) Cedric Maxwell
   b) Robert Parish
   c) Don Nelson
   d) Ed Macauley

QUESTION 244: On April 12, 1990, in a 139-118 win over the Miami Heat, the Celtics' shots were falling. They hit 62.2% from the field and made all of their foul shots. Six different players made all of their free throws including Larry Bird and Kevin McHale who both were 10 for 10. How many foul shots did the Celtics make to set the team record for the most made without any misses?
   a) 33
   b) 34
   c) 35
   d) 36

QUESTION 245: During the 1980s and early 90s a ticket to a Celtics game at the Boston Garden was the toughest ticket in town. Every game sold out between December 1980 and the Celtics final contest at the Garden on May 5, 1995. How many consecutive sellouts did the Celtics achieve at the Boston Garden?

    a) 662
    b) 667
    c) 670
    d) 677

MISCELLANEOUS

QUESTION 246: In the 1950 NBA Draft Red Auerbach and the Boston Celtics made history. They selected Chuck Cooper in the second-round, the first African American player ever chosen in the NBA Draft. What college did Cooper attend before joining the Celtics?

    a) Pittsburgh
    b) Duquesne
    c) Virginia
    d) West Virginia

QUESTION 247: The Boston Celtics were a high scoring, fast break team in the 1950s. They led the league in scoring eight times in nine seasons from 1952 to 1960. In one of those years they set the team record for scoring with 124.5 points per game, which at the time was also the league record. What Celtics team holds the team record with 124.5 points per game?

    a) 1952-53
    b) 1955-56
    c) 1958-59
    d) 1959-60

QUESTION 248: In 1978 the Celtics were part of one of the most unusual transactions in the history of professional sports. The Celtics and the San Diego Clippers made a swap of seven players, two draft picks, and owners. What former Celtics

owner essentially "traded" the team in order to become the owner of the San Diego Clippers franchise?
a) Irv Levin
b) Walter A. Brown
c) Paul Gaston
d) Harry T. Mangurian, Jr.

QUESTION 249: The Celtics have played for 63 seasons and more than 5,000 games including the playoffs. But their first season didn't start so well. They lost the first five games in franchise history, won a game and then lost another five straight to start the 1946-47 season at 1-10. What was the first team that lost to the Celtics on November 16, 1946?
a) Cleveland Rebels
b) New York Knickerbockers
c) Pittsburgh Ironmen
d) Toronto Huskies

QUESTION 250: The Celtics have always been considered one of the greatest home teams in the history of professional sports. They've only had one season where they actually won more away games than home games. This one season came *after* they won a title and in a year where they *didn't* win it all. What is the only Celtics team to win more games on the road than at home?
a) 1974-75
b) 1981-82
c) 1984-85
d) 2008-09

Bonus: Red Auerbach Fill in the Blank Quote

Bonus Question 5: "Show me a good loser and I'll show you a" ... what?
   a) loser
   b) Laker
   c) bad winner
   d) opponent

Bonus Question 6: Okay, so this one isn't a quote by Red . . . *but it certainly qualifies as trivia!* What current Celtics player was born nine days after the author of this book?
   a) Kevin Garnett
   b) Paul Pierce
   c) Ray Allen
   d) Brian Scalabrine

Chapter Five Answer Key

Time to find out how you did – put a check mark next to the questions you answered correctly, and when you are done be sure and add up your score to find out your Playoffs IQ!

THE NUMBERS GAME
__ Question 201: B
__ Question 202: C
__ Question 203: B
__ Question 204: D
__ Question 205: B

THE ROOKIES
__ Question 206: D
__ Question 207: B
__ Question 208: A
__ Question 209: A
__ Question 210: A

THE VETERANS
__ Question 211: A
__ Question 212: D
__ Question 213: D
__ Question 214: C
__ Question 215: C

THE LEGENDS
__ Question 216: B
__ Question 217: D
__ Question 218: D
__ Question 219: A
__ Question 220: C

THE GUARDS
__ Question 221: C
__ Question 222: D
__ Question 223: B
__ Question 224: D
__ Question 225: D

THE BIG MEN
__ Question 226: B
__ Question 227: B
__ Question 228: D
__ Question 229: D
__ Question 230: A

THE COACHES
__ Question 231: D
__ Question 232: B
__ Question 233: A
__ Question 234: C
__ Question 235: A

THE PLAYOFFS
__ Question 236: D
__ Question 237: C
__ Question 238: C
__ Question 239: B
__ Question 240: D

THE FABULOUS FEATS
   _ Question 241: A
   _ Question 242: B
   _ Question 243: B
   _ Question 244: C
   _ Question 245: A

MISCELLANEOUS
   _ Question 246: B
   _ Question 247: D
   _ Question 248: A
   _ Question 249: D
   _ Question 250: A

BONUS QUESTION 5: A
BONUS QUESTION 6: B

Got your Playoffs total? Here's how it breaks down – check the scale to find out how well you carried the club throughout the Playoffs . . . and the coach who best represents your score!

RED AUERBACH	= 45-50
KC JONES	= 40-44
TOM HEINSOHN	= 35-39
CHRIS FORD	= 30-34
RICK PITINO	= 00-29

Think you can do better next season? Well, you're going to get a shot at it – be on the lookout for Boston Celtics IQ, Volume II!

About the Author

David Colburn is a computer programmer and lifelong Celtics fan. He is what would be considered a sports statistics and information "nut." Since 2002, he has meticulously maintained his website, celticstats.com, which is home to a staggering amount of data on Celtics players, coaches and seasons. In his spare time, he plays Ultimate Frisbee around New England and follows his other favorite teams. Additionally, this Vermont native has recently relocated to Massachusetts in order to catch the action live at the TD Garden. He is a co-author of the upcoming Sports by the Numbers book, *Boston Celtics: An Interactive Guide to the World of Sports*.

Visit David on the web at: www.celticstats.com

References

BOOKS
Boston Celtics Encyclopedia: Peter C. Bjarkman (1999)
Sporting News Official 2001-02 NBA Guide (2001)
Sporting News Official 2006-07 NBA Guide (2006)

DVDS
Boston Celtics – The Complete History: NBA Dynasty Series DVD
    set (2004)

WEBSITES
Baseball-reference.com
Basketball-reference.com
Basketball.ballparks.com
Celticstats.com
Databasebasketball.com
Hoophall.com
NBA.com

Sports by the Numbers

The award-winning Sports by the Numbers book series is a proud sponsor of Black Mesa's IQ books. SBTN is the series where every number tells a story—and whether you're a beginning fan just learning the ropes, or a diehard fanatic hanging on the outcome of every game, the crew at SBTN have got you covered.

Check out Sports by the Numbers on the web:

www.sportsbythenumbers.com

Current titles include:

- *University of Oklahoma Football*
- *University of Georgia Football*
- *Major League Baseball*
- *New York Yankees*
- *Boston Red Sox*
- *San Francisco Giants*
- *Mixed Martial Arts*
- *NASCAR*

For information about special discounts for bulk purchases, please email:

sales@savasbeatie.com

Sports by the Numbers Praise

"You think you know it all? Not so fast. To unearth fact upon fact about this historic franchise in a unique yet tangible way is an impressive feat, which is why the following pages are more than worthwhile for every member of that cult known as Red Sox Nation . . . This is a book that Red Sox fans of all ages and types will enjoy and absorb."
— Ian Browne, Boston Red Sox Beat Writer, MLB.com

"Fighting is physical storytelling where villains and heroes emerge, but the back-story is what makes the sport something that persisted from B.C. times to what we know it as today. Antonio Rodrigo Nogueira living through a childhood coma only to demonstrate equal grit inside the ring on his way to two world championships. Randy Couture defying age like it was as natural as sunrise on his way to six world championships. The achievements are endless in nature, but thanks to this book, these great human narratives are translated into a universal language—numbers—in a universal medium—fighting."
— Danny Acosta, Sherdog.com and *Fight!* Magazine Writer

"Statistics have long been resigned to slower, contemplative sports. Finally, they get a crack at the world's fastest sport in this fascinating piece of MMA analysis."
— Ben Zeidler, CagePotato.com, *Fight!* Magazine

"Long-time Sooner fans will revel in the flood of memories that flow from these pages. You'll think back to a defining moment—that favorite player, an afternoon next to the radio, or that special day at Owen Field. And the information contained here is so thorough that you'll relive those memories many times."
　　— Bob Stoops, Head Coach, University of Oklahoma
　　Football

"*University of Oklahoma Football – S*ports By The Numbers is a must read for all OU Football junkies. I read trivia I didn't know or had forgotten."
　　— Barry Switzer, Legendary Head Coach, University of
　　Oklahoma Football

"Clever and insightful. For fans who don't know much about the history of stock-car racing, it's like taking the green flag."
　　— Monte Dutton, best-selling NASCAR author

"You will find the most important numbers that every fan should know, like Joe DiMaggio's 56-game hitting streak, Ted Williams' .406 batting average, Hank Aaron's 755 homeruns, and Nolan Ryan's seven no-hitters, but there are hundreds of lesser-known stats. Even if you think you know everything about baseball, I guarantee you will learn a whole lot from this book."
　　— Zack Hample, best-selling author of *Watching Baseball*
　　Smarter

"This book is fascinating and informative. If you love Yankees trivia, this is the reference for you."
　　— Jane Heller, best-selling novelist, Yankees blogger, and
　　author of *Confessions of a She-Fan: The Course of True Love*
　　with the New York Yankees

"This book brings you tons of info on America's best loved and most hated team—the New York Yankees . . . a great book for any age or fan of America's Game and Team. A must read."
— Phil Speranza, author of the *2000 Yankee Encyclopedia 5th edition*

"I loved this book. I could not put it down at night. This book is the perfect bedside or coffee table reading material. *New York Yankees: An Interactive Guide to the World of Sports* has a huge collection of interesting data about the entire New York Yankees history."
— Sam Hendricks, author of *Fantasy Football Guidebook* and *Fantasy Football Almanac 2009*

"The Yankees matter—but you already knew that, and soon, you will dive into this wonderful yield by the good folks at Sports by the Numbers and you will lose yourself in baseball, in history, in numbers, and in the New York Yankees. I envy you. I can't think of a better way to pass the next couple of hours."
— Mike Vaccaro, best-selling author and award-winning columnist for the *New York Post*

Black Mesa Titles

Look for these other titles in the IQ Series:

- *Mixed Martial Arts*
- *Atlanta Braves*
- *Boston Red Sox*
- *Cincinnati Reds*
- *Milwaukee Brewers*
- *St. Louis Cardinals*
- *New York Yankees*
- *University of Oklahoma Football*
- *University of Georgia Football*
- *University of Florida Football*
- *Penn State Football*
- *San Francisco 49ers*

Look for your favorite MLB and collegiate teams in Black Mesa's *If I was the Bat Boy* series, and look for your favorite NFL and collegiate teams in Black Mesa's *How to Build the Perfect Player* series, both by award-winning artist and author Cameron Silver.

For information about special discounts for bulk purchases, please email: black.mesa.publishing@gmail.com

Praise for MMA IQ

"Every time I work on a cut I am being tested and I feel confident I can pass the test. After reading MMA IQ I'm not so sure I can do the same with this book."
— UFC Cutman Jacob "Stitch" Duran,
www.stitchdurangear.com

"MMA fans everywhere pay attention—this is your best chance to reign supreme in your favorite bar stool. The trivia and stories come at you so fast and so furious you'll wish Stitch Duran was in your corner getting you ready to do battle."
— Sam Hendricks, award-winning author of *Fantasy Football Tips: 201 Ways to Win through Player Rankings, Cheat Sheets and Better Drafting*

"From the rookie fan to the pound for pound trivia champs, MMA IQ has something that will challenge the wide spectrum of fans that follow the sport."
— Robert Joyner, www.mmapayout.com

"I thought I knew MMA, but this book took my MMA IQ to a whole new level . . . fun read, highly recommended."
— William Li, www.findmmagym.com

You can visit *Mixed Martial Arts IQ* author Zac Robinson on the web:

www.sportsbythenumbersmma.com
www.cutmanstitchduran.com

Praise for NY Yankees IQ

"If you consider yourself a tested veteran at baseball trivia in general or a hardcore expert at Yankees trivia in particular, it doesn't matter—you owe it to yourself to test your skills with this IQ book, because only when you pass this test can you truly claim to be a cut above everyone else."

— Daniel J. Brush, award-winning author of *New York Yankees: An Interactive Guide to the World of Sports*

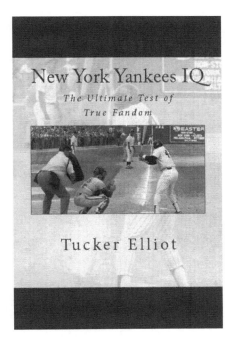

Praise for Atlanta Braves IQ

"There are just two Hall of Famers who really know the Braves road from Boston to Milwaukee to Atlanta—Eddie Mathews and Braves IQ! This book will determine if you can win fourteen-straight division titles or if you will get lost trying to get off I-285. If you're a Braves fan or you know a Braves fan, this is a must-have."

— Dr. Keith Gaddie, award-winning broadcast journalist and author of *University of Georgia Football: An Interactive Guide to the World of Sports*

Praise for Boston Red Sox IQ

"The author of two dozen books on the Boston Red Sox, Bill Nowlin challenges every member of Red Sox Nation to step up to the plate and prove your mad-trivia skills. This book, however, is much more than a test of your fandom—it is a celebration of the many legends who have made the Boston Red Sox one of the most beloved franchises in the history of sport."

   — Daniel J. Brush, award-winning co-author of the Sports by the Numbers series

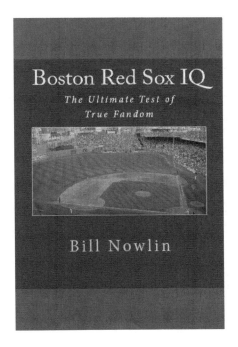

27342742R10068

Made in the USA
Middletown, DE
15 December 2015